Naturopathic Medicine Marketing

How to Become the #1 Go-To ND in Your Area

Lori Werner and Sherry Sbraccia

Naturopathic Medicine Marketing: How to Become the #1 Go-To ND in Your Area
Copyright © 2024 by Lori Werner - Sherry Sbraccia

All rights reserved. No part of this book may be reproduced or transmitted in any form or by any means, electronic or mechanical, including photocopying, recording, or by any information storage and retrieval system, without permission in writing from the author.

This book is not intended to provide medical advice. The information contained in this book is intended to help healthcare providers improve their marketing strategies and is not a substitute for professional medical advice, diagnosis, or treatment.

Cover design by Sherry Sbraccia
Interior design and typesetting by Sherry Sbraccia

ISBN: 9798882625282
Printed in the United States of America

There is no guarantee associated with the contents of the book. Results will vary and we are not held liable for any damages directly or indirectly in result from the material.

Dear Reader,

We are thrilled to introduce "Naturopathic Medicine Marketing: How to Become the #1 Go-To ND in Your Area and are so glad you have decided to take this marketing journey with us!

We understand the unique challenges and opportunities that come with running a health practice. We have combined our knowledge to provide you with practical strategies and actionable tips to help you reach more people and make a difference in their health journeys.

Whether you are just starting out or looking to take your practice to the next level, this book is a must-read for any natural doctor who is passionate about helping people. We hope you enjoy reading it as much as we enjoyed creating it.

Sincerely,

Lori Werner

Sherry Sbraccia

Introduction: The Power of Naturopathic Medicine Marketing

In the ever-evolving landscape of healthcare, the role of naturopathic providers is more crucial than ever. As an ND, you possess a unique opportunity to not only enhance the well-being of your patients but also to establish yourself as the go-to expert in your community.

In this book, we embark on a journey together, exploring the strategic and practical aspects of Naturopathic Medicine Marketing. We will delve into the art of identifying your ideal patient, building trust through leveraging your credentials, awards and board certifications, and leveraging patient-education based marketing strategies.

Each chapter is designed to equip you with actionable insights and proven strategies, empowering you to rise above the competition and claim your position as the #1 Naturopathic Doctor in your area.

Are you ready to transform your practice and leave an indelible mark on the world of naturopathic health? Let's begin the adventure of becoming the preferred choice for patients seeking compassionate and expert care.

This book is not just about high-level strategies; it's about providing you with specific, implementable actions to distinguish yourself in the competitive healthcare landscape. Are you ready to unlock the secrets that will propel your practice to new heights? Let's dive in.

Allow us to introduce the dynamic duo behind "Naturopathic Medicine Marketing: How to Become the #1 Go-To ND in Your Area." This book is a collaborative effort led by Lori Werner, the founder of Medical Marketing Whiz, along with her esteemed colleague, Sherry Sbraccia.

Lori Werner is the driving force behind this comprehensive guide. As the founder of Medical Marketing Whiz, Lori brings her passion for empowering private practice physicians to the forefront. With over 20 years experience in healthcare marketing, she has dedicated herself to helping naturopathic physicians navigate the complexities of marketing.

Sherry Sbraccia, a key team leader at Medical Marketing Whiz, plays a vital role in the success of the book. With a profound understanding of healthcare marketing strategies, Sherry contributes her expertise to ensure the content is not only insightful but also actionable. Her commitment to staying ahead of the marketing curve is reflected in the strategies presented in this book.

Together, Lori and Sherry form a powerhouse team committed to delivering valuable content that will guide you on your journey to becoming the #1 naturopathic medicine provider in your area. Get ready to benefit from their collective wisdom and experience as you embark on this transformative adventure.

Naturopathic Medicine Marketing
How to Become the #1 Go-To ND in Your Area

Table of Contents

Chapter 1: Unveiling the Foundations of Successful ND Marketing

Chapter 2: Evaluating and Transforming Your Marketing Approach

Chapter 3: How Patients Choose a Doctor & Defining Your Ideal Patient

Chapter 4: Your Website: Position Yourself As the Authority in Naturopathic Medicine

Chapter 5: Local SEO for NDs: Google Business and Online Listings

Chapter 6: Your Online Reputation & Why It Matters

Chapter 7: Social Media Mastery for Naturopathic Doctors

Chapter 8: Email Marketing: Leveraging the Goldmine Within Your Practice

Chapter 9: The Power of Webinars: Educate & Attract New Patients

Chapter 10: Healthful Gatherings: Mastering In-Office Events for Naturopathic Doctors

Chapter 11: Podcasting for NDs: Amplifying Influence Beyond the Microphone

Chapter 12: Promotional Calendar of Ideas for Naturopathic Doctors

Conclusion: Your Journey to Becoming the #1 Naturopathic Doctor in Your Area

Bonus Material

Scan the QR code for FREE 30 DAY access.
Use Code: LADYDOC

Are you a healthcare provider searching for an affordable and efficient way to enhance your marketing efforts?

Look no further than the DR. MARKETING TOOLKIT
The ultimate do-it-yourself program designed specifically for doctors like you.

Inside the Dr. Marketing Toolkit, you'll discover a treasure trove of invaluable resources that will equip your staff with the skills and knowledge they need to drive your practice's success. From insightful training videos to ready-to-use Canva templates, email marketing templates, and webinar PowerPoint slide decks – we've got you covered.

Scan the QR code to set up a free demonstration

Schedule 30 Days of Social Media Posts In Under 10 Minutes

With hundreds of libraries and content available at the tips of your fingers, you can schedule a month's worth of content in just 10 minutes or less across multiple social media platforms including Facebook, Instagram, LinkedIn, and your Google Business Profile.

Chapter 1

Chapter 1: Unveiling the Foundations of Successful Naturopathic Medicine Marketing

Welcome to the journey of discovering the secrets to marketing your practice effectively and attracting your ideal patients—the patients you genuinely enjoy helping with their wellness, health, and prevention. In this chapter, we'll unravel the four key secrets that will pave the way for you to become the #1 naturopathic health provider in your area.

Before diving into the secrets, let's lay the groundwork by emphasizing the importance of leveraging all the things that make you the best choice for wellness and prevention.

Having the best training, treatment options, and staff is commendable, but it's not enough for people to choose you as their provider. Patients have to see you as the expert for their particular symptom or condition. They need to view you as someone who has the experience, authority and credibility to solve their healthcare concerns.

Patients don't easily switch doctors, especially when it comes to long-standing relationships with healthcare providers. Personally, I can attest to this reality, having been under the care of my internist for over 15 years. The familiarity and trust built over time with a particular physician makes the decision to transition to a new practitioner a considerable challenge, particularly because naturopathic medicine isn't covered by my insurance (in my area).

Existing patients often have a strong bond with their current providers. To entice them to consider your services, they must view you as the expert addressing their unique health concerns—issues their current doctor may not even be discussing.

Allow me to share a personal experience that highlights this dilemma. As a business owner and busy mom and wife, you can imagine my life is quite stressful. The cumulative stress of running my business, mentoring my team, mom duties, and caring for my aging parents brought me to the breaking point. In my 30s it seemed like I could handle stress pretty well, being able to juggle multiple things at once. But once I hit 40 that all changed.

I talked to my internal medicine doctor who offered me Klonopin to take as needed. But then I looked at all the side effects and really didn't want to take it.

One day, I received an email from an ND that really spoke to me. It was about natural solutions for stressed out business owners. Me exactly! I scheduled a virtual visit with him to find out what it was all about.

After talking with Dr. Mike, I learned about naturopathic medicine and biofeedback and how I can address my symptoms through naturopathic medicine. He talked to me about how entrepreneurs prioritize their business over their health until it catches up to them and they can no longer work on the business... because of this, a lot of the high achievers that come to him are dealing with stress, insomnia, & focus issues. Yes! This doctor understood exactly what I was dealing with and wanted to help me get to the root cause of my stress and offered me customized protocol that I could take action on.

This process left me pondering why my longtime internist hadn't offered me anything expect a prescription. There was no conversation about why I was feeling so burned out and stressed and how I could change that. I was so thankful Dr. Mike reached out to me via email.

This story underscores the importance of not only offering naturopathic medicine solutions, but also ensuring that potential patients are aware of alternatives to traditional medicine and pharmceuticals. People actively seek solutions to their health problems, but the challenge lies in making them aware that you provide a holistic approach to their whole health and can help them heal in a natural way.

Furthermore, it's crucial to acknowledge the competitive landscape in healthcare. Numerous providers offer similar services, making it imperative for you to stand out. As we delve into the four secrets of naturopathic medicine marketing in this book, remember that your investment in time, training, and technology equips you with the skills and desire to make a significant impact. Yet, it's equally important to convey this wealth of expertise to both your community and your current patients.

Marketing starts from within

Before we set sail into the vast seas of marketing strategies, it's crucial to anchor our journey with a fundamental truth: effective marketing starts from within. Your practice is not just a physical space where patient consultations are conducted; it is a dynamic ecosystem fueled by the energy, expertise, and enthusiasm of your team.

Your office is not just a physical (or virtual) space; it's a living, breathing entity that can either hinder or amplify your marketing efforts. The demeanor of your staff, the follow up messages that are sent, and the efficiency of your processes—all are integral components of the patient journey. Thus, before delving into external marketing strategies, we must first transform our offices into thriving, welcoming hubs.

Hiring the A-Team: Your Office Ambassadors

Your team is not just a collection of professionals; they are ambassadors for your practice. Each team member, from the front desk to the medical staff, contributes to the narrative that patients carry with them. A well-chosen, trained, and motivated team can turn your office into a magnet for patient loyalty and positive word-of-mouth marketing.

Motivating your staff members and keeping them motivated can be a significant challenge. However, it is an essential part of operating any successful business and it should not be ignored. Motivation is a direct link to job performance. Individuals and teams that are motivated achieve individual, group and overall business goals. In addition, motivated individuals consistently deliver a high-quality work performance, are more apt to overcome obstacles and challenges, and are more productive with their time.

Motivating your staff requires effective, dynamic leadership, which is not something you do "to" your staff, it is something you do "with" them. Some keys to effective leadership include:

Integrity:
- Leading with integrity by modeling the behavior you want others to display.
- Setting standards that are clearly communicated and measurable, and then training, coaching, and motivating to those standards maintains a culture of integrity.
- Leading with integrity builds trust. Show the staff that you trust them by creating a culture of self-responsibility; encourage them to solve problems, contribute to building the practice, organize and implement new procedures, and handle day-to-day challenges.

Partnership:
- Build relationships with your staff by sharing the big picture and by positively emphasizing the importance of their role in achieving it.
- Coaching helps to build partnerships. This is not about discipline, it is about encouraging your staff members to discover their best and perform at it.

- One way for a staff member to contribute to the big picture is to develop and grow. Ask staff members to stretch beyond what you have observed them doing in the past and provide them opportunities for growth with advanced education, training, and special projects.

Affirmation:
- Observe the good in the staff and offer praise and affirmation.
- Reward the team for their contributions.
- Learn what staff members feel positive about doing and maximize their opportunity to contribute in these areas.
- Create opportunities to communicate with your staff members.

Rewards and Incentives:
For a reward and incentive programs to be effective, clear and measurable performance goals must be set. These goals must also be clearly communicated with the team with details such as the time period within which the goal should be achieved, and how the goal will be measured. Lastly, and most importantly, ongoing encouragement, motivation and coaching (as needed) should be provided to support the staff in goal achievement.

Rewards for achieving goals, contributing new ideas, or for solving problems is a great way to keep the staff motivated.

One way to reward your staff is to offer treatments/supplements at cost or at no charge. This is a terrific incentive and it allows staff members to experience the program so they can better service your patients. However, some staff members may not be interested and, therefore, the reward will not be of value to them. Take the time to understand what would be a good incentive for each individual in your office.

Of course, you can't diminish the importance of showing employee appreciation. Acknowledging excellent performance is best done with a sincere "thank you." You might send a personal note or stop by the employee's desk to convey your appreciation.

Meetings:

Regular staff meetings are important in developing and maintaining motivation. In busy practices, it is often difficult to find time to communicate new information or to feel "connected" to the staff. Meetings provide this opportunity and allow for the staff to communicate with you and with each other without the distraction of the bustling practice.

Meetings can be used in many ways. Every meeting does not have to have the same purpose or agenda, and can be used for a number of reasons including:

- To update the staff on changes in the practice and to communicate new information.
- To address and solve a problem.
- To celebrate a recent success.
- To plan an upcoming event.
- To conduct a training.
- To demonstrate a new or existing treatment or procedure to increase staff knowledge.
- To review and refresh on existing policies and procedures.

Some tips on conducting a successful meeting include:
- Keep agendas manageable in scope. The entire agenda should be covered during the allocated time.
- Be prepared. Outline the agenda and the goals of the meeting.
- Clearly communicate the date, time and meeting place in advance to give staff time to plan.
- Assign a "scribe" who will take notes and distribute minutes to the staff.
- Be mindful of maintaining an open forum for comments, questions and suggestions, while making sure to stay on time and topic. For items that require more time, recommend they be added to an agenda for a future meeting.
- Meetings should be upbeat, relaxed and comfortable.
- End the meeting on time.
- Have the "scribe "post minutes so that any action items assigned, deci-

sions made, or information dispelled are clearly documented.
- All action items should be put on the next agenda for follow up.

Crafting the Marketing Environment: Action Items

Office Evaluation:

- Conduct a thorough assessment of your office environment. From the waiting area to the treatment rooms, identify areas for improvement.
- Develop a step-by-step plan to address and enhance each aspect of your office environment.
- Plan and rehearse your office tour. Ensure that every team member is familiar with the process and can showcase your practice seamlessly.
- Experience your practice from a patient's perspective. Look up your practice online, scrutinize your Google listing, evaluate your website, and call the office incognito.
- Analyze the patient experience from the first phone call to leaving the office. Identify areas for improvement in the online and offline patient journey.

Injecting Fun into the Office

What is the vibe at your office? The happiness within your walls radiates onto your patients. The attitude of your staff sets the tone for the patient experience. A team with a positive attitude is your best marketing asset. Patients not only seek medical expertise but also yearn for a comforting, enjoyable atmosphere. Make the extra effort to infuse happiness into every interaction, and watch it transform into a powerful marketing tool.

"A team with a great attitude is the best marketing there is".

As we embark on this chapter, let's embrace the transformative power of our office environments. Crafting a positive, inviting space is not just a marketing strategy—it's a commitment to the well-being and satisfaction of every patient who walks through your doors.

Chapter 2

Evaluating and Transforming Your Marketing Approach

Let's delve into the common missteps Naturopathic Medicine Doctors may encounter and navigate the dynamic shift from traditional to contemporary marketing approaches.

Recognizing Marketing Missteps

Misstep 1: *Introducing New Services Without a Confident Marketing Strategy*
Embracing new services is a thrilling venture, but without a robust marketing strategy, your cutting-edge therapies might end up as mere dust collectors.

Before investing in new equipment or extensive training, it's crucial to have a solid marketing plan in place. Don't let your valuable investments become overlooked assets. Ensure you have a strategy to inform both existing patients and the broader community about your new services.

In the upcoming sections, we'll explore strategies to bolster your confidence in marketing new services, ensuring that your investments contribute to the growth and success of your practice.

Misstep 2: *Past Marketing Attempts that Yielded Disappointing Results*
Many NDs find themselves in a frustrating cycle—having invested in marketing initiatives that either failed to deliver results or, worse, turned out to be a rip-off. This disillusionment often stems from experiences with marketing agencies, where doctors may hop from one agency to another without seeing any tangible outcomes.

Some physicians may have worked with agencies claiming local expertise, but fall short in understanding the nuances of the healthcare space, especially in the field of naturopathic medicine. Picture an agency marketing not only your practice but also the local restaurant, tire store, and plumber. Such agencies lack the specialized knowledge required for naturopathic medicine.

This disillusionment can lead doctors to feel they've squandered both time and money. The frustration reaches a point where they contemplate abandoning marketing efforts altogether, thinking, "to heck with it." It's crucial to recognize that not all marketing approaches are created equal, and the key lies in partnering with a specialized agency that understands naturopathic medicine marketing intricately.

In the upcoming sections, we'll delve into insider tips that we implement for our clients—NDs—ensuring you gain insights tailored to the unique demands of naturopathic health patients. Let's navigate the world of effective and specialized marketing strategies together.

Misstep 3: *Overworked Staff with Limited Marketing Expertise*
Another common misstep involves relying on staff members to handle your practice's marketing, often on top of their existing responsibilities. Your staff may find themselves wearing multiple hats, such as being a receptionist, nurse or office manager, all while being tasked with marketing duties. Despite their dedication, they may lack true marketing expertise.

This situation often results in what I like to call "kind-of sort-of marketing." Your staff may be doing a bit of marketing, but it occurs sporadically, squeezed in between their numerous other responsibilities. The outcome is only partial results, and, in reality, no actual cost savings. In fact, this approach tends to make your staff less efficient in their primary roles.

It's essential to recognize that expecting your staff to effectively market your practice while juggling a myriad of other responsibilities is an unrealistic demand. In the upcoming sections, we'll discuss strategies to empower your staff and streamline your marketing efforts without compromising their efficiency in their primary roles.

Old School vs. New School Marketing: Navigating the Shifting Terrain

In the realm of Naturopathic Medicine Marketing, many NDs have traditionally leaned on "old school" strategies, such as relying solely on their website and keywords as the primary marketing tool. It's a "sit around and hope people find you" strategy. While effective for patients actively searching with specific keywords, it doesn't necessarily position you as a top-of-mind or community leader. Moreover, it may not reach those potential patients who are unaware that natural solutions to their symptoms exist. To truly stand out, it's essential to position yourself as a leader in your community, offering specialized wellness and prevention services that set you apart.

To establish yourself as the undisputed #1 go-to Naturopathic Doctor in your area, a focused and consistent approach is paramount. By honing in on four key strategies every quarter, you'll set in motion a powerful marketing engine designed to attract, nurture, and convert leads, ultimately solidifying your authority in health and wellness.

1) Local SEO Mastery
The first pillar of your marketing engine is Local SEO. This involves optimizing your Google Business profile to ensure it vividly reflects the comprehensive range of services you offer. When someone searches for a "naturopathic doctor near me" or a "holistic medicine doctor near me," your goal is to be the top result. This entails not only being discovered but being chosen. How? By amassing a trove of 5-star reviews. These reviews not

only testify to your excellence, but also significantly impact your Google ranking. We'll explore strategies to secure a prominent position in local search results and create a reputation that precedes you.

2) Social Media Mastery
The second key component is Social Media Mastery. This goes beyond the conventional use of social platforms. We'll dive deep into leveraging social media to educate patients, showcase your expertise, and highlight your specialized services. Imagine creating an environment where patients feel like they know you intimately even before setting foot in your office. Additionally, we'll unravel the secrets of targeted social media campaigns tailored to attract your ideal patient demographic. Get ready to transform your social media presence into a dynamic tool that not only engages but converts.

3) Email Marketing Mastery
Email Marketing takes the third spot in our quartet of strategies. It's not just about sending emails; it's about staying top of mind with your patients and list every single month. We'll guide you on crafting emails that make your patients feel cared for, dedicated to educating them on the latest advancements in natural medicine and prevention. Beyond patient engagement, we'll explore how email marketing can fill your events, webinars, increase social media followers, and gather more reviews. Prepare to wield email marketing as a multifaceted tool that drives patient loyalty and amplifies your reach.

4) Patient Education Marketing Mastery
The fourth and final piece of your marketing engine is Patient Education Marketing. This encompasses webinars, events, and podcasts—the highest conversion mechanisms in the realm of marketing. We'll delve into how these platforms not only educate but also forge a deep connection with your audience. Patient education becomes the catalyst for trust, making your practice the natural choice for those seeking a naturopathic medicine approach.

In the upcoming sections, we'll break down each of these strategies, providing you with actionable insights to implement every quarter. This is about creating a marketing engine that not only attracts and retains patients but positions you as the unrivaled leader in Naturopathic Medicine. It's time to propel your practice to new heights by mastering these essential components of naturopathic medicine marketing.

Chapter 3

How Patients Choose a Doctor & Defining Your Ideal Patient

Let's get into the mindset of how patients go about choosing a naturopathic health provider. Word-of-mouth is still king. Most patients are going to ask their friends and family to see who they recommend. If they move to a new area, they often join local community forums like Facebook Groups and post that they are looking for a wellness provider and see who people recommend in the comments. As a Naturopathic Medicine Doctor, your aim is to be the resounding #1 recommended ND in your area.

Yet, in the modern healthcare narrative, even word-of-mouth ends up going online. After a recommendation, prospective patients head to Google to research the provider and to get the phone number or website to make an online appointment.

On Google, they will research the recommended doctor, but also usually look at the top 2-3 other providers. They may compare you to Functional Medicine doctors, Holistic Medicine, Wellness Coaches, or traditional internists to see who seems to provide the best alternative medicine treatment options. They read the Google reviews and compare each doctor. They are looking for validation that the recommended provider is in fact the right choice and is worth them taking time out of their busy day to make an appointment. Reviews become the crescendo of trust. They are also a huge factor in search ranking on Google.

Simultaneously, patients seek assurance in your expertise and authority. They are looking for a doctor who doesn't just treat symptoms but comprehensively solves their problems. What does your online presence convey? Is your website all stock photography or does it showcase your expertise, your team, your awards, certifications, and credentials?

Next up is the way you communicate. Is your communication style part of your online marketing strategy so potential patients can get to know and connect with you? Patients want to feel a connection with their provider as someone that will not only listen to them but is an expert in solving their issues.

Understanding how patients decide isn't just strategy; it's your backstage pass to being not just seen but chosen. In the next section, we're diving into finding your ideal patient—an essential step in making sure your practice takes the lead role in their healthcare story.

Unveiling Your Ideal Patient Avatar
Alright, let's talk about something crucial: understanding who your ideal patients are. It's not just about offering advanced services and top-notch care; it's about making sure your marketing connects with patients with the exact patient who needs your services most.

Before you unleash your marketing strategy, you need to identify:
WHO your ideal patient is
WHERE they hang out online
WHAT symptoms or health concerns they're facing

Knowing your ideal patient:
- Guides your social media strategy, helping you create posts, videos, and lead magnets that draw in more leads and patients.
- Influences your understanding of your patients' needs, steering you toward new devices and services that cater to those needs.

- Crafts your offers and promotions, speaking directly to your avatar's problems and motivating them to schedule an appointment.
- Boosts your email marketing effectiveness, leading to higher open rates, better conversion rates, and even specific campaigns tailored to different avatars.
- Helps you discover which paid platforms you should run ads on — and what targeting options you should use

Demographics: The Avatar Blueprint:
Applying demographic information breathes life into your patient avatar. Gender, age range, ethnicity, marital status, age of children, annual household income, education level, radius around your office, target cities, hobbies, and interests—all these elements build a vibrant picture of your ideal patient.

These demographic details aren't just for show; they're the backbone of your targeted marketing efforts. Whether you're delving into Facebook & Instagram Ads or developing a lead magnet or e-book, your patient avatar's demographics are your guiding stars.

Example Avatar:
Meet Julie, a college-educated 47-year-old woman. She's married and has two kids, one in college and the other in high school. She and her husband own their home, with an annual household income of over $150,000. She is health-conscious and a follower of Dr. Mark Hyman, loves Whole Foods, Trader Joe's, and her Peloton bike. But, Julie has recently been frustrated with increased fatigue, weight gain, bloating, and a slow digestive system. Her doctor has only given her pharmaceuticals as treatment options After talking to a few girlfriends, Julie goes to Google and looks up "Gut Health" and 'Leaky Gut' to do some research on what could be going on.

See how much easier it is to craft a marketing campaign if you're speaking to a patient like Julie? Your messages will resonate with her.

Now, grab that Patient Avatar Worksheet, and let's embark on the journey of defining your ideal patient avatar. Trust me; when you're clear on who your patients are, delivering a message that sparks action becomes a breeze.

Patient Avatar Worksheet:

Gender:

Age Range:

Ethnicity:

Marital Status:

Age of Children:

Annual Household Income:

Level of Education:

Radius around your office:

Cities to target:

Hobbies & Interests:

Chapter 4

Your Website - Position Yourself as the Authority in Patient's Health

Your website stands as the virtual gateway to your practice, a powerful tool to establish credibility, foster trust, and engage with your target audience effectively. Tailoring your website to the specific field of Naturopathic Medicine requires careful consideration of both structure and content. Beyond the fundamental pages, this chapter delves into essential elements that can elevate your online presence.

So, what pages should your website have? What navigation structure should you create? These are the core pages.

Home
About Us
Our Services
Conditions Treated
Reviews and Testimonials
Blog
Contact Us

The home page should immediately position you as an expert. Infuse personality through genuine photos and videos, showcasing your team, office, and equipment. Avoid generic stock photos for a more relatable and trustworthy online presence.

Under the hero image on the website, position yourself as an expert by prominently featuring logos of affiliations like AANP, A4M, OncANP, BCB, EndoANP, and other relevant credentials. Furthermore, you should highlight logos of awards received, such as Top Docs Award, Best of City Award, or any other recognition, fostering a positive perception of your practice. This is a critical component to build trust and is shown to increase conversions on your website by up to 48%.

The home page should also feature social media links to Facebook, Instagram, and LinkedIn, enabling visitors to engage with your practice on various platforms.

Within "About Us," you might incorporate a drop-down menu for subcategories including "Meet the Team," "Why Choose Our Practice," etc. This provides visitors with a more profound understanding of your practice.

Address recruitment challenges by featuring a "Careers" page under the "About Us" section. Potential candidates can learn more about your practice and even submit applications online.

Our Services Page: Optimize user experience by including a dropdown listing the various services offered. You should have an individual page for every service that you provide. This is critical for enhancing visibility and search engine optimization.

Conditions Treated: This is an opportunity for potential patients to find their symptom and learn the various treatment options that are available to them. For example, a page about metabolic issues could cover everything from diabetes and obesity to thyroid disorders, elevated cholesterol and PCOS.

A page on autoimmune disorders would feature Rheumatoid Arthritis, Psoriatic Arthritis, Psoriasis, Lupus, Ulcerative Colitis, Crohn's Disease, Addison's Disease, Graves' Disease,
Hashimoto's and more. Write the copy in patient-friendly language rather than medical terminology.

Reviews and Testimonials: Dedicate a page to showcase patient feedback, including reviews from external sites like Google and Yelp. Authenticity in testimonials fosters trust.

Critical Page Elements
Clear Business Description: Ensure a succinct and compelling description above the fold, capturing visitors' attention within seconds.

Primary Contact Details: Display a prominent phone number in the upper right-hand corner of every page, encouraging immediate contact for services.

Call to Action: Facilitate easy requests by offering a web form for quote inquiries, catering to visitors with various preferences for communication.

Online Presence Enhancement:
Mobile-Friendly Design: Cater to the growing number of users accessing websites via smartphones by ensuring a condensed, mobile-ready version of your site, facilitating easy navigation and contact.

In essence, your website serves as a dynamic tool to not only inform but also impress potential patients, positioning you as a top-tier healthcare provider in the field of naturopathic medicine. By incorporating these elements, Naturopathic Medicine Doctors can create a robust online presence that resonates with authenticity, expertise, and patient-centric values.

Chapter 5

Local SEO for NDs: Google Business and Online Listings

Let's dig into the nitty-gritty of local search engine optimization (SEO) — your ticket to being the top choice in your community for naturopathic health. We're breaking it down into the Google Business profile, online listings, and the golden nugget—your online reputation.

Local SEO, or search engine optimization, is your key to getting noticed in your community. Imagine it as your digital billboard attracting patients in your area. Getting listed on the first page of Google for "Your City + Naturopathic practitioner" comes down to four primary factors:

1. Having a claimed and verified Google Business Profile Listing
2. Having an optimized Google Business Profile for your local area
3. Having a consistent N.A.P. (Name, Address, Phone Number Profile) across the web so that Google feels confident that you are a legitimate organization located in the place you have listed and serving the market you claim to serve.
4. Having reviews from your patients in your service area

If you have each of these four factors working in your favor you will SIGNIFICANTLY improve the probability of ranking on page one of Google in your market.

How to establish a strong Name, Address, Phone Number Profile

One crucial element of your local SEO is maintaining a consistent Name, Address, Phone Number (N.A.P.) profile across the web, especially for optimizing your ranking on Google Business.

Google recognizes a consistent N.A.P. as a signal of authority, making it imperative for every ND to establish a strong foundation. Before diving into claiming your Google Business Profile and building out your other online directory listings, start by defining your authentic N.A.P. Ensure that it is uniformly referenced across various online platforms.

Consistency, in this context, means always using the legitimate name of your practice. For instance, if your clinic is "Main Street Naturopathic Medicine" consistently list it as such, avoiding variations like "Main St. Naturopathic Medicine" Be cautious of misinformation suggesting keyword stuffing in your business name. While it may have been effective in the past, it now violates Google's policies.

Maintain uniformity across all directory sources by listing your exact company name, using the same primary business phone number, and presenting your address consistently. Avoid the temptation to assign unique phone numbers to each directory; this only confuses your online profile.

When it comes to directory listings, utilize your primary phone number, the original business name, and the principal address consistently. For instance, if your clinic is situated at "1367 South West 87th Street, Suite Number 105," ensure it is listed exactly the same way on every platform.

Pay attention to the finer details to achieve a seamless name/address profile across the web. Avoid inconsistencies like using "South West" in one place and "SW" in another. Precision is key.

To discern your N.A.P. from Google's perspective, conduct a search for

"Your Office" and analyze the references on Google Maps. Compare this with high-authority sites like YP.com, Yelp.com, and Healthgrades. Identify the prevalent combination of N.A.P. and adopt it consistently for all future directory work.

Remember, in the world of Naturopathic Medicine Marketing, attention to detail and a cohesive online identity can be the key to attracting the right patients and establishing your practice as a trusted authority.

Next, we are going to unlock the full potential of your practice with the Google Business Profile— a powerful and FREE tool that enhances your online presence, engages potential patients, and boosts your visibility in local searches.

Google Business Profile (GBP):

When someone in your community is searching for a Naturopathic Medicine Doctor, 93% of the time, they will click on one of the top three listings that pop up on Google. Think of it like this: imagine you're craving pizza and you search for "pizza near me." You're likely to choose from the first three pizza places that show up, right? It's the same for patients looking for healthcare services.

For you, as a Naturopathic Medicine Doctor, this means that securing a spot in the Google Three Pack is like having a backstage pass to patient choices. Patients are highly likely to contact and choose a healthcare provider from this exclusive trio. So, when your practice shines in that top three, you're not just visible—you're the go-to choice for patients in your area. It's not just crucial; it's the golden ticket to being their preferred healthcare destination.

Getting into the Google 3-Pack involves optimizing your online presence, specifically your Google Business profile. Here are key steps to increase your chances of securing a spot:

Claim and Optimize Your Google Business Profile:

Below you will find a step-by-step guide for checking, claiming, and managing your Local Business Listings on Google.

1. Go to https://www.google.com/business/

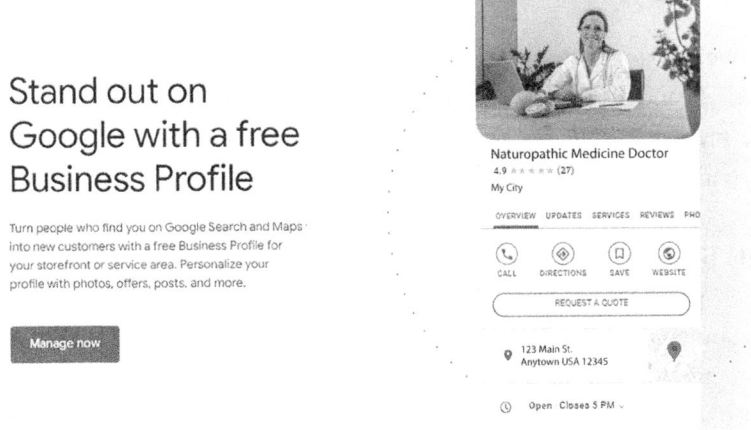

2. Claim your business

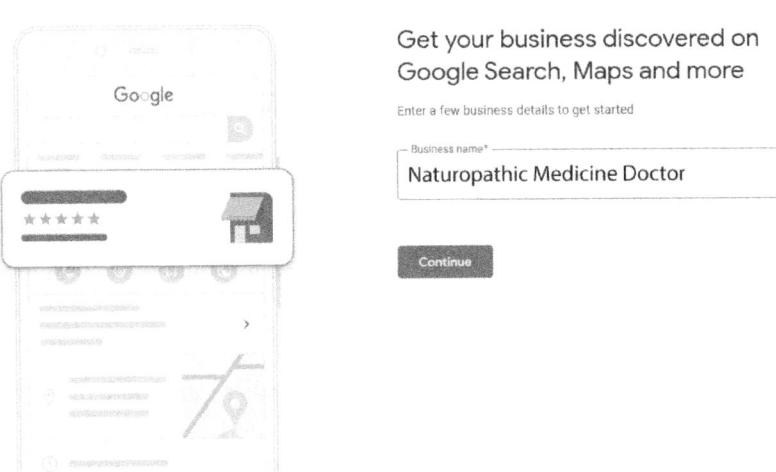

3. Enter your business address and all pertinent information

4. Choose a verification method
- By postcard
- By phone
- By email
- Instant verification
- Bulk verification

5. Once your listings are claimed, go to your Google Business Profile Dashboard and fill in all the necessary information to optimize your profile.

Update Your Company Name to Read "Company Name" – e.g. "Main Street Naturopathic Medicine". Don't add any additional keywords here. Add your Website Address – This will create an important inbound link Add a detailed business description that highlights your services and specialties, and what sets your practice apart. Be sure to write the description in patient-friendly language, avoiding medical jargon. Naturally incorporate local keywords in your description to enhance local search visibility. Next, choose primary and secondary categories that accurately represent your services. Consider the specific specialties you offer within patients's health such as Naturopathic practitioner, Alternative medicine, Holistic medicine, and more. You will choose one primary category and can add up to nine secondary categories.

List Your Core Services and Products:
Clearly outline the primary services you offer, such as gut health, nutritional therapy, botanical medicine, and lifestyle management, and be sure to specify any unique or specialized services that distinguish your practice. If applicable, feature products related to patients's health, such as supplements or wellness items, and clearly describe the benefits of each product. Don't forget to incorporate keywords in your descriptions to enhance local search visibility.

Business Hours:
Double-check that your business hours are accurate, including any variations for specific days or services. Update hours promptly for holidays or

special occasions when the office may be closed.

Phone Number:
Use a local number (not an 800 number), and make sure it is your real office number rather than a tracking number. We find that 800 numbers don't rank well. If you use a tracking number, it won't be consistent with your other online directory listings and will result in poor ranking.

Upload Photos -AS MANY AS POSSIBLE:
Google values businesses that provide a rich and informative experience for users, and an extensive collection of high-quality photos contributes significantly to this. A study conducted by Google found that businesses with photos receive 42% more requests for directions and 35% more click-throughs to their websites. This data underscores the impact of visual content on user engagement. Google's algorithm interprets a robust gallery of photos as a positive signal, signaling to the search engine that your business is active, reputable, and deserving of higher visibility. Therefore, regularly updating and diversifying your photo library not only enhances the user experience but also positively influences your position in local search results.

Add high-quality images that reflect the welcoming atmosphere of your practice. Include photos of the exterior, waiting area, examination rooms, equipment, and staff. Feature images that highlight your team's expertise and compassionate care. Consider, including photos and brief bios of key team members, fostering a personal connection with patients.
You can also create geo context for the photos by uploading them to a video sharing site like Panoramio.com (a Google Property) that enables you to Geo Tag your photos to your company's location.

Upload VIDEOS:
They don't have to be professionally produced and will resonate well with your potential patients. A best practice is to upload the videos to YouTube and then Geo Tag them using the advanced settings.Leveraging your Google Business Profile as a platform for educational content is a strategic move that can significantly benefit naturopathic doctors. By incorporating

informative videos within your profile, you have the opportunity to directly engage with potential patients and showcase your expertise.

Consider creating videos that delve into common patients's health topics or introduce new services, offering valuable insights that resonate with your target audience. Video content serves as a powerful tool for humanizing your practice, allowing potential patients to connect with you on a personal level before even stepping into the office. This human touch builds trust and familiarity, essential elements in the decision-making process for individuals seeking patients's health services. Moreover, providing educational content on your Google Business Profile demonstrates your commitment to patient education and positions you as a knowledgeable and approachable healthcare provider in the eyes of your community.

Business Attributes:
Google Business Profile attributes play a crucial role in shaping the identity and visibility of your patients's health practice. Adding business attributes to your Google Business Profile such as patients-owned, veteran-owned, black-owned, and Latino-owned not only contributes to the diversity and inclusivity of your profile but also holds the potential to boost your practice's visibility on Google.

Incorporating these attributes in your profile signals to Google that your business aligns with specific categories, making it eligible for inclusion in searches that prioritize diversity. Google recognizes the importance of diverse representation, and having these attributes can give your practice a boost in relevant searches. It's a powerful way to highlight the unique aspects of your patients's health services and the inclusive nature of your practice.

Potential patients actively seek healthcare providers who resonate with their values, and Google's acknowledgment of these attributes enhances your chances of standing out. This recognition not only fosters a sense of community and connection but also contributes to creating a healthcare landscape that reflects the diversity of the patient population. So, embrace and proudly display these attributes on your Google Business Profile to make a positive impact on both your practice and the broader healthcare community.

You can maximize the potential of your Google Business Profile by leveraging some of Google My Business features like posts, Q&A, and appointment booking. Regularly update your profile with informative and engaging posts to keep it active and relevant. Share updates on new services, health tips, or upcoming events to showcase your expertise and maintain patient interest. Utilize the Q&A section to address common queries and provide valuable information, demonstrating your commitment to patient education. Additionally, enable appointment booking directly through your Google My Business listing, streamlining the patient journey and making it convenient for them to connect with your practice.

By actively utilizing these features, you enhance your online presence, engage with your audience, and make it easier for potential patients to choose your Naturopathic Medicine practice for their healthcare needs.

Remember, being a Naturopathic Medicine Doctor is not just a label; it's a dynamic force that can set you apart in the competitive healthcare landscape. Embrace it on your Google Business Profile, and let your practice shine as a beacon of excellence in patients's health.

Beyond Google Business Profile - Online Directory Listings

Enhancing your practice's visual appeal extends beyond Google Business. There are hundreds of other online business directory listings that are critical for local SEO including an array of platforms such as Apple Maps, Waze, Yelp, Bing, Mapquest, Facebook, Instagram, and even voice-activated systems like Siri and Alexa.

Online directory listings for doctors serve as powerful sources of backlinks, significantly enhancing the overall Search Engine Optimization (SEO) standing. These listings act as digital checkpoints, each providing a valuable link back to the doctor's website. Search engines, recognizing these backlinks as credible endorsements, assign higher authority to the website. As the website's authority increases, so does its visibility in search engine results.

For NDs navigating the competitive online landscape, these backlinks from diverse directories, mapping systems, and social media platforms not only amplify the practice's digital footprint but also contribute substantially to elevating its SEO profile. The interconnected web of listings, when optimized strategically, weaves a robust fabric of backlinks, ensuring that the ND's online presence stands out prominently in relevant search queries, ultimately attracting more patients to the practice.

Picture this scenario: A prospective patient searches for a new holistic health provider using their car's navigation system, relying on Apple Maps or Waze. Ensuring accurate information across these platforms is paramount. Unbeknownst to many, online directory listings play pivotal roles in various scenarios, from a doctor changing locations to office closures on holidays.

Imagine the frustration when a patient follows the directions provided by a navigation app in their car, only to end up at an outdated address due to a recent office move. Navigating practice relocations requires meticulous attention to updating information across diverse platforms. Be it Apple Maps, Google Maps, or Waze, accuracy in your practice's location is non-negotiable to prevent inconvenience and uphold your professional image.

Patients also rely on voice-activated systems like Siri or Alexa in their searches for doctors and other healthcare providers. A misstep in updating this information can result in patients showing up at closed practices, leading to dissatisfaction and potentially negative reviews.

What about all of the nutriceuticals you have in your practice and the different procedures you offer? Most of the nutraceutical companies have a "find-a-physician" section on their websites. Are you listed as a provider on their website? Reach out to your reps and make sure they have submitted you to their physician finder directories!

Online listings are susceptible to user-generated suggestions and edits. From phone number changes to category modifications, Naturopathic Medicine Doctors must be vigilant in accepting or rejecting these proposals. A proactive approach ensures the preservation of accurate information, thwarting potential disruptions caused by erroneous suggestions.

As an ND, orchestrating a symphony of online listings demands consistency. From your business name to categories and descriptions, maintaining uniformity across diverse platforms ensures a harmonious online presence. Consistency not only aids in search engine rankings but also eliminates confusion among potential patients seeking holistic healthcare services.

The journey of managing online directory listings transcends mere setup—it demands ongoing optimization and active maintenance. Regularly updating office hours, reviewing and responding to suggested edits, and staying attuned to patient reviews are integral components of a proactive strategy. This continuous commitment safeguards your online reputation and ensures accurate information dissemination.

In conclusion, Naturopathic Medicine Doctors embarking on the digital journey must broaden their perspective beyond Google's horizon. Navigating the diverse panorama of online directory listings, encompassing mapping systems, voice-activated platforms, and social media directories, is a strategic imperative. As the orchestrator of your online presence, embrace consistency, respond adeptly to reviews, and actively maintain your digital presence to stand tall in the competitive healthcare landscape.

Chapter 6

Your Online Reputation & Why It Matters

Patients who are seeking preventive healthcare, in particular, conduct thorough research when selecting healthcare providers, making online reviews a valuable resource in their decision-making process. It's essential for NDs to actively manage their online reputation, encourage positive reviews, and address any concerns to meet the expectations of this informed patient demographic.

While other review platforms like RealPatientRatings.com exist, the reality is that the majority of patients turn to Google when evaluating and selecting a doctor. It's crucial for naturopathic doctors to prioritize soliciting reviews on the Google Business Profile specifically, given its widespread usage and impact on local search visibility. Additionally, Yelp serves as a valuable secondary option, catering to those who may not have a Gmail email address, a requirement for leaving Google reviews. By strategically focusing efforts on these prominent platforms, naturopathic medicine doctors can maximize their online presence and effectively engage with prospective patients.

Google reviews also contribute significantly to the search engine optimization (SEO) of an NDS online presence. Positive reviews signal credibility and relevance to search engines, improving the chances of ranking higher in search results. This visibility is paramount for attracting new patients, especially in the competitive field of holistic medicine.

For patients navigating the complex landscape of healthcare choices, trust is paramount. Positive Google reviews act as real-life testimonials, offering reassurance to potential patients. They highlight the quality of care, communication style, and overall patient experience, making it easier for patients to make informed decisions about their healthcare providers.

Investing in marketing efforts without managing online reputation can create a bottleneck in converting potential patients into new appointments. A robust online presence, fueled by positive Google reviews, not only complements marketing strategies but also serves as a foundational element for patient conversion.

Getting Reviews

With that said, how can you get reviews? What kind of process will you need to actually get reviews from your happy patients?

5 Free Strategies to Generate More Google Reviews:

QR Codes: Create a QR code that links to your Google Business Profile review URL. You can find this link inside your Google Business Profile. Etsy has some really nice signs that you can have made with a custom QR code. Place the signs at the checkout area, allowing patients to easily leave reviews by scanning the code. This provides a convenient and immediate way for satisfied patients to share their experiences.

Staff Engagement: Create a small business card size card with your Google Review QR code link. You can make these easily on Canva.com for free and have them printed at your local Fed Ex Office or on Vistaprint.com. Empower your front desk staff to ask patients about their experience during checkout. If positive, encourage them to scan the QR code for a Google review, creating a seamless process.

Social Media Testimonials: Leverage your social media platforms to showcase patient testimonials. Once a week post a patient testimonial on Facebook, Instagram, and LinkedIn and Include your Google review link in posts, encouraging followers to share their positive experiences online.

Webinar Reviews: At the end of your patient education webinars (more on those later in this book), ask viewers to leave you a review if they enjoyed the webinar presentation.

Email and SMS Campaigns: Implement automated email and SMS campaigns post-appointment, seeking patient feedback. For those expressing satisfaction, provide a direct link to leave a Google review.

Simple Steps To Use When Asking For Reviews

1. Ask the patient if they will do you a favor and write a review.
2. Tell them it will take less than 5 min.
3. Explain how your practice and others in the community would benefit from a review.
4. Tell them the easiest way to write a review (use their phone, or click a link in an email you will send)
5. Thank them and let them know you look forward to reading their comments.

Sample Scenario Script

Once you or your staff member asks the patient for a review, this is how you can follow through with the process to make sure you get one.

The medical assistant walks the patient to the front counter after the appointment is complete and says the following to the front-desk staff member:

Medical assistant: Cindy has offered to write a review for us. Will you please give her one of our Review Cards so she can post one on Google, Yelp, or Facebook?

(Have your staff member show the patient how to scan the QR code).

Front Desk Staff: Thank you so much for offering to write a review, Cindy. I know Dr. Jones is looking forward to reading your comments.

Patient: Sure (Scans QR code)

Front Desk Staff: Thanks again for agreeing to post a review, it really means a lot to us and to our reputation for you to share your opinion of our office online. Do you have any questions about the process I can answer?

Proceeds with the rest of the normal check-out process.

Using Email To Get More Reviews

To get a nice little bump in the number of reviews that you have, you should develop an email list of your friends, family, and patients who have been with you for quite some time. People that you know, like, and trust, who would be willing to act on your behalf.

Put together that email list in an Excel sheet. It might be ten contacts, or it might be 700 contacts. Include the names and email addresses of these people. Then, use a tool like Constant Contact or MailChimp or another email marketing tool to send an email blast with the following message:

Subject: Your Feedback Matters – Share Your Experience with [Doctor's Name]

Dear [Patient's Name],

I hope this email finds you well. At [Name of ND office], we are committed to providing exceptional care and continuously strive to enhance the patient experience. We value your opinion and would greatly appreciate it if you could take a few moments to share your experience with us.

Your feedback not only helps us maintain the high standard of care we aim for but also assists other individuals in choosing the right naturopathic provider for their needs. We believe in the power of shared experiences, and your review can make a significant impact.

To leave a review, simply click on the following link: [Insert Google Review Link]

Thank you for being a part of the [Name of ND office] community. Your insights are instrumental in helping us continually enhance our services.

Best regards,

[ND Name]
[Your Title/Role]
[Website]
[Contact Information]

Responding to reviews

When someone leaves you a review on Google, you are able to see it and respond. Timely review monitoring is crucial. Responding to reviews, especially negative ones, within 24-48 hours demonstrates a commitment to patient satisfaction.

Since you're a healthcare professional, it's a little trickier than just simply responding. You are under HIPAA regulations and are not allowed to reveal any personal information about patients. Because of this, you need to be very careful of how you respond, whether to a negative or positive review.

There are some essential things to remember when responding to reviews as a Naturopathic Healthcare professional:

- Never include the patient's name in your response.
- Never include any other information identifying them, such as where they live, their job, or even their gender.

- The response should not discuss why they were at your office, including any treatments they received, what brought them into your office, or the time they were seen—it should be generic.

Example Responses to Positive Reviews

"Thank you for sharing your review! We strive to provide the best possible care to every patient, and always enjoy reading about a good experience."

"Wow – thanks for your kind remarks! We thrive on this type of feedback, so we'll be sure to pass this review off to the team. Thanks again!"

"Thank you for this feedback. Our practice has an amazing group of providers and staff, and we all take great pride in our work."

"Thank you for taking the time to share this review! We take great pride in providing exceptional care to all of our patients and appreciate your kind words."

Example Responses to Negative Reviews

"Our policy is to schedule plenty of time between patients in order to avoid long waits. We strive to deliver the best care possible to all our patients, but we occasionally fall behind schedule because of emergencies. We value your feedback and want to thank you for taking the time to share it. You can call our office and ask for our Office Manager [NAME] if you have any further comments or suggestions."

"Thank you for taking the time to provide feedback. We strive to make each patient's experience exceptional, and it pains us to hear if we fall short of a patient's expectations. Please call our office at (XXX) XXX-XXXX to discuss this matter further."

"Thank you for bringing this to our attention. We take all feedback seriously. As a healthcare provider, we are bound by HIPAA regulations and cannot discuss any specific patient information in a public forum. We encourage you to contact us directly to discuss your concerns further. We value our patients and their feedback, and we hope to have the opportunity to address any issues and improve your experience with our practice."

Google reviews are not just testimonials but pivotal elements in a comprehensive digital marketing strategy. For patients seeking holistic healthcare, positive reviews instill confidence, making your practice stand out and reinforcing the trustworthiness that every patient seeks in their healthcare journey.

In the next chapter, we're diving into social media—the heartbeat of your online engagement. Let's go!

Chapter 7

Social Media Mastery for Naturopathic Medicine

In the dynamic landscape of naturopathic medicine marketing, social media has emerged as a powerful tool, particularly with providers specializing in holistic health, integrative medicine, or preventative medicine. Social media is not merely a platform; it's a dynamic space for Naturopathic Medicine Doctors to amplify their influence, foster patient relationships, and curate a distinctive online presence. As we delve deeper into the realms of social media marketing, remember that authenticity, engagement, and education form the cornerstone of your digital success.

Let's explore the myriad benefits that a dedicated business page on social media brings:

A Window to Professional Excellence:
Your social media business pages serve as a digital canvas where you can showcase the essence of your naturopathic medicine practice. Unlike personal profiles, a business page empowers you to share educational content, impactful videos, health tips, and essential information about your office.

Unlock the "Recommendation" Advantage:
One of the notable features of social media business pages is the invalu-

able "recommendation" feature. This element amplifies the voice of satisfied patients, providing a genuine endorsement that resonates with your audience.

Behind-the-Scenes Connection:
Social media serves as the backstage pass for patients to glimpse the inner workings of your medical practice. It's a platform to convey the personality behind the brand, the spectrum of services offered, and the specialized expertise that defines your practice.

Consistency with Branding and Website:
Your social media business pages should seamlessly align with your branding and website. Ensure comprehensive listings of the services you provide, accompanied by regular content updates. Consistency fosters engagement, building a loyal following over time.

Educational and Personal Harmony:
Striking a balance between educational and personal content is key. Avoid the pitfall of transforming your social media into a sales pitch. Instead, share content that educates, resonates, and provides a personal touch. Remember, social media is a narrative, not a sales brochure.

Platforms like Facebook, Instagram, YouTube, LinkedIn, and TikTok offer unique opportunities to connect with a diverse audience, share valuable information, and ultimately attract new patients.

Next, let's explore the benefits and strategies specific to each platform.

Facebook: Connecting with the Community

Why Facebook Matters:
Women dominate the usage of Facebook, posting four times more frequently than men. For Naturopathic Medicine Doctors, this means a significant portion of your target audience is actively engaged on this platform. Establishing a Facebook business page allows you to share educational content, health tips, and behind-the-scenes glimpses of your practice.

Benefits:
Educational Content: Share articles, videos, and infographics to educate your audience about how NDs treat the whole person by identifying underlying causes and offering herbal medicine, nutritional therapy, and massage therapy, in addition to counseling and stress reduction techniques.

Recommendation Feature: Leverage the "recommendation" feature to build trust, as positive reviews can influence potential patients.

Brand Visibility: Provide a window into your practice, showcasing your brand, services, and expertise.

The Power of Local Facebook Groups

In the realm of social media, Facebook stands out as a community powerhouse, and within this vast network lies a goldmine for doctors aiming to connect with local patients. The secret? Local Facebook groups. These digital spaces have become hubs of community interaction, providing a unique opportunity for Naturopathic Medicine Doctors to network with local patients and position themselves as more than just a healthcare provider. You become a trusted member of the community, fostering trust and credibility that extends beyond the digital realm.

1. Finding Your Niche:
Before diving into the world of local Facebook groups, identify the specific niche or demographic you want to target. Whether it's nutrition, wellness, or specific health concerns, pinpointing your focus will guide you to the right groups.

2. Joining Local patients-Centric Groups:
Facebook groups centered around patients's interests, local events, or general community life are abundant. Use Facebook's search feature to find groups in your area, ensuring they are active and have a significant number of members. Keywords like "local," "community," or the name of your city can narrow down the search.

3. Observe, Engage, Connect:

Once you've joined relevant groups, take time to observe the dynamics. Understand the interests, concerns, and conversations that resonate within the community. Engage authentically by participating in discussions, offering valuable insights, or even seeking advice where appropriate.

4. Promoting Your Events and Webinars:

Local Facebook groups provide an ideal platform to promote events and webinars tailored to naturopathic medicine. However, it's crucial to do this strategically. Rather than bombarding groups with promotional content, share valuable information, and occasionally highlight upcoming events. Create posts that spark interest and invite participation.

5. Collaborating with Group Administrators:

Forge partnerships with group administrators to ensure your engagement aligns with the group's guidelines. Administrators can be valuable allies in amplifying your message and events within the community.

6. Utilizing Facebook Group Features:

Make use of group features like announcements and events to highlight your practice. When used judiciously, these features can draw attention without coming across as overly promotional.

7. Monitoring and Adjusting:

Regularly monitor the group dynamics and adjust your approach based on feedback and interactions. Flexibility is key in adapting to the evolving needs and interests of the community.

Local Facebook groups offer a dynamic space for Naturopathic Medicine Doctors to not only promote their events and webinars but also to immerse themselves in the pulse of the local community. Embrace the power of connection, and let these digital communities become an extension of your practice's welcoming environment.

Instagram: Visual Storytelling for Wellness & Prevention

With its emphasis on visual content, Instagram is ideal for Naturopathic Medicine Doctors. Patients are drawn to this platform, creating an opportunity for NDs to showcase their expertise and personality.

Understanding the differences between posts, reels, and stories is crucial for creating a well-rounded and effective Instagram strategy:

1. Instagram Post:
- Format: Static images or videos (up to 60 seconds).
- Purpose: Posts are the main content on your profile. They can showcase your services, share educational content, highlight patient testimonials, or provide updates about your practice.

Tips:
- Use high-quality visuals and captivating captions.
- Incorporate relevant hashtags to increase discoverability.
- Include a call-to-action (CTA) to encourage engagement, such as asking followers to share their experiences or tag friends.

2. Instagram Reel:
- Format: Short-form videos (up to 60 seconds).
- Purpose: Reels are a way to create fun and engaging content. They can include educational snippets, behind-the-scenes looks, or even showcase your personality to connect with your audience.

Tips:
- Leverage trends and challenges to increase visibility.
- Keep it concise and visually dynamic to capture attention quickly.
- Add music or voiceovers to enhance engagement.

3. Instagram Story:
- Format: Vertical images or videos (up to 15 seconds per segment).
- Purpose: Stories are temporary, allowing for more casual, real-time updates. They're perfect for sharing day-in-the-life content, event promotions, or time-sensitive announcements.

Tips:
- Use features like polls, quizzes, and questions to encourage interaction.
- Share behind-the-scenes content to humanize your practice.
- Utilize the "Swipe Up" feature (if available) for direct links to your website or event pages.

Tips for Naturopathic Medicine Doctors Using Instagram:

Visual Consistency:
- Maintain a consistent visual style and color palette to create a cohesive and recognizable brand aesthetic.

Educational Content:
- Share bite-sized educational content related to naturopathic medicine. Break down complex topics into easily digestible information.

Patient Stories and Testimonials:
- Feature patient success stories (with consent) to build trust and credibility. Personal narratives resonate well with audiences.

Interactive Content:
- Use interactive features like polls, quizzes, and surveys to engage with your audience and gather insights.

Timely and Relevant Content:
- Stay updated with current health trends and share timely information. This positions you as a knowledgeable and responsive healthcare provider.

Event Promotion:
- Promote in-office events, webinars, or healthful gatherings through posts, stories, and reels. Create anticipation and excitement among your followers.

Community Engagement:
- Engage with your community by responding to comments, direct mes-

sages, and participating in relevant conversations.

Consistent Posting Schedule:
- Establish a consistent posting schedule to keep your audience engaged. Use Instagram Insights to determine optimal posting times.

By leveraging the unique features of posts, reels, and stories, Naturopathic Medicine Doctors can create a well-rounded Instagram presence that resonates with their audience and attracts new patients. Regularly analyzing performance metrics and adapting your strategy based on audience feedback will contribute to ongoing success on the platform.

YouTube: Education through Video Content

Creating a YouTube channel can be a powerful strategy to enhance online presence, educate patients, and improve Google search ranking. Here's why and how Naturopathic Medicine Doctors can benefit from having a YouTube channel.

Visual Education:
- YouTube allows NDs to create visually engaging content to educate patients about various patients's health topics. Videos can cover a range of subjects, from preventive care and lifestyle tips to explaining lab testing and treatment options.

Patient Engagement:
- Video content is highly engaging and can help build a stronger connection with patients. By offering valuable information in an accessible format, NDs can foster a sense of trust and credibility, leading to increased patient engagement.

Improved Google Search Ranking:
- Google, the world's largest search engine, owns YouTube. When you create and optimize videos with relevant keywords and descriptions, it positively impacts your overall online visibility. YouTube videos often appear in Google search results, contributing to a higher search

ranking for your practice.

Reach a Wider Audience:
- YouTube has over 2 billion logged-in monthly users, and a significant portion of them are patients. Creating content tailored to your target audience can help you reach a wider demographic and attract new patients.

Healthcare Trends on YouTube:
- Healthcare content on YouTube has been on the rise, with an increasing number of people turning to the platform for holistic health-related information. According to a Think with Google study, over 68% of YouTube users watch videos to learn about something they're interested in, including health and wellness.

Educational Series and Webinars:
- Naturopathic Doctors can use YouTube to host educational series and webinars on various health topics. This positions you as an authority in your field and provides a platform for viewers to ask questions or seek clarification.

Testimonials and Success Stories:
- Share patient testimonials and success stories (with proper consent and privacy considerations) through video. Positive experiences from real patients can influence potential patients and build trust in your services.

Collaborate with Influencers:
- Consider collaborating with healthcare influencers or experts in related fields to create joint content. This can expand your reach and bring credibility to your channel.

YouTube Analytics Insights:
- YouTube provides analytics tools that offer insights into viewer demographics, watch time, and engagement. By analyzing these metrics, NDs can refine their content strategy to better meet the needs and pref-

erences of their audience.

Mobile Accessibility:
- With the increasing use of mobile devices, YouTube is a platform that caters to on-the-go users. Patients can access your videos from their smartphones, making it a convenient way to consume health-related information.

A YouTube channel can be a valuable addition to your online marketing strategy. It not only allows for patient education and engagement but also contributes to improved search rankings, making your practice more discoverable online. As the trend of seeking healthcare information on YouTube continues to grow, establishing a presence on this platform becomes increasingly important for Naturopathic Doctors.

LinkedIn: Professional Networking and Expertise Showcase

LinkedIn is a powerful platform for naturopathic health doctors to build a professional network, connect with potential patients and members of professional organizations such as AANP, and engage with nutriceutical companies. Here are some best practices for utilizing LinkedIn effectively:

Optimize Your Profile:
- Ensure that your LinkedIn profile is complete and presents a professional image. Use a high-quality photo, write a compelling headline, and include a detailed summary that highlights your expertise in naturopathic medicine.

Highlight Holistic Health Expertise:
- Clearly articulate your specialization in holistic health in your profile summary and experience sections. Use relevant keywords to make your profile easily discoverable by individuals looking for naturopathic or preventive health services.

Connect with Other Healthcare Professionals:
- Actively connect with other healthcare professionals, especially those who may refer patients to your practice. Personalize connection requests with a brief message expressing your interest in collaboration.

Engage in LinkedIn Groups:
- Join and participate in LinkedIn groups related to holistic health, alternative medicine, nutrition, and your specific healthcare interests. Engaging in group discussions can help you connect with peers, share insights, and stay updated on industry trends.

Share Educational Content:
- Share articles, research, and educational content related to naturopathic medicine. This positions you as a thought leader in your field and keeps your network informed about the latest developments.

Connect with Professional Patients:
- Identify and connect with professional patients in various industries, as they may be potential patients or valuable connections. Engage with their content, participate in relevant discussions, and share insights related to whole body health.

Showcase Patient Success Stories (with Consent):
- Highlight patient success stories, with proper consent and privacy considerations, to showcase the positive impact of your preventative and holistic approach to healthcare. This humanizes your practice and builds trust.

Publish Articles and Updates:
- Share your expertise by publishing articles or regular updates on LinkedIn. This content can range from insights into complementary and alternative medicine.

Use LinkedIn Ads Strategically:
- Consider using targeted LinkedIn ads to reach specific professional demographics, such as nutritionists or professional patients in your

region. LinkedIn's advertising platform allows you to customize your audience for maximum impact.

By incorporating these best practices, Naturopathic Doctors can leverage LinkedIn to expand their professional network, increase visibility in the industry, and connect with valuable stakeholders.

TikTok: Capturing Attention with Creativity

TikTok has become a powerful platform for content creators, including NDs, to engage with a wide audience. While the primary nature of TikTok is entertainment, many healthcare professionals have successfully utilized the platform to educate, share insights, and even attract patients. Here's a look at how doctors are using TikTok:

Educational Content:
- NDS can leverage TikTok to share short, informative videos on health topics. These videos often break down complex medical information into digestible and engaging content.

Myth-Busting:
- Addressing common misconceptions or debunking health-related myths can be an effective way for NDs to establish themselves as credible sources of information.

Personalized Insights:
- Some doctors share behind-the-scenes glimpses of their daily work, humanizing the medical profession. This can help build a connection with the audience and demystify the healthcare experience.

Challenges and Trends:
- Participating in TikTok challenges and trends within the healthcare community can increase visibility. This could involve joining broader trends or creating challenges related to health and wellness.

Patient Testimonials (with Consent):
- With proper consent and privacy considerations, NDs might share patient success stories or testimonials. This can humanize the practice and demonstrate real-world positive outcomes.

Q&A Sessions:
- Hosting question-and-answer sessions allows NDs to directly engage with their audience, addressing common health concerns and establishing themselves as approachable experts.

Leveraging Humor:
- Incorporating humor into healthcare-related content can make it more shareable and relatable. However, it's crucial to balance entertainment with accuracy and sensitivity.

Promotion of Services and Events:
- NDs can use TikTok to promote health-related events, webinars, or new services. This can create awareness and attract a younger demographic who may not engage with traditional marketing channels.

It's important to note that TikTok's audience tends to be younger, so the effectiveness of attracting patients may vary based on the target demographic. Additionally, maintaining professionalism and adhering to ethical guidelines is paramount when sharing medical content on any platform. While TikTok can be a valuable tool for building an online presence, its role in attracting patients should be part of a broader digital marketing strategy that includes other platforms and channels.

10 Strategies for Success on All Platforms:

1. Ensure your social media pages align with your practice's branding and website.

2. The 80/20 Rule: Adhere to the golden rule of social media posting – 80% dedicated to valuable, educational, and personal content; the remaining 20% or less reserved for promotional or special announce-

ments. This balance cultivates an authentic connection with your audience.

3. Engagement is Key: Actively respond to comments, messages, and reviews. Use social media as a platform to engage, not just broadcast.

4. Post regularly, ideally at least a few times a week. You can pre-schedule your posts! Your content should include photos and videos of the doctor or staff, inspirational quotes, educational posts, testimonials, before & after photos, and other things that will be engaging for your audience.

5. Invite your friends to follow your pages and ask your staff to do the same. You need to click the "Invite Friends to Like the Page" and select friends in your area. Share your content to your personal profiles.

6. Get your staff involved! Each staff member should be expected to follow the social media pages and participate in the success of your social media, which includes promoting the page and participating in the behind-the-scenes posts. Ask your staff to share at least one post per week on their personal social media channels.

7. Make it someone's job (or hire a marketing agency) - not the doctor or your college-age kid - to check Facebook & Instagram daily and respond to any comments or direct messages. This person should also be responsible for consistently coming up with new, engaging content.

8. Follow the social media pages of other local businesses. Engage with their posts by commenting on their content a few times per week. If you expect people to engage with your content, you also need to engage with other people's content!

9. Try some promotions or contests to get people to like your pages.

10. Learn the basics of social media marketing for doctors with our Social Media 101 Training and Instagram 101 Training. (available on the www.medicalmarketingwhiz.com website under Social Media Marketing).

20 Social Media Story or Reel Ideas for Naturopathic Medicine Doctors:

1. Behind the Scenes: Take your audience behind the scenes of your daily life at the clinic (or telehealth), showcasing your team and workspace.

2. Patient Success Stories: Share brief testimonials or success stories (with permission) to build trust and show the positive impact of your services.

3. Day in the Life: Document a day in your life to give followers a glimpse into the routine of your day.

4. Medical Myth Busting: Debunk common myths or misconceptions related to health and wellness.

5. Healthcare News Updates: Share updates on the latest healthcare news, breakthroughs, or research relevant to your field.

6. Mental Health Tips: Share advice on maintaining mental health and managing stress.

7. Community Involvement: Highlight any community events, health fairs, or workshops you're involved in.

8. Seasonal Health Tips: Share health tips and advice that are relevant to the current season.

9. Naturopathic Doctor's Recommended Reads: Share book recommendations related to health, wellness, or personal development.

10. Flashback Friday: Share throwback videos or images from significant moments in your ND career.

11. Wellness Wednesday: Use Wednesdays to share content focused on overall wellness, including physical and mental health.

12. Wellness Checkup Guide: Explain the importance of regular wellness checkups and what to expect during the visit.

13. Hormonal Health Explained: Break down common hormonal issues in patients and their impact on overall health.

14. Mental Health: Discuss the intersection of mental health and patients's health, offering tips for well-being.

15. Navigating Menopause: Provide guidance on managing symptoms and maintaining health during menopause the natural way.

16. Understanding Thyroid Health: Break down the complexities of thyroid health and offer practical advice for maintaining it.

17. Gut-Brain Connection: Explain the connection between gut health and hormonal balance, and suggest ways to support both.

18. Stress and Hormones: Discuss the impact of stress on hormonal health and strategies to manage stress effectively.

19. Sleep: Offer tips for improving sleep quality.

20. Highlight the Integration of Technology and Natural Health: Share a post discussing how biofeedback wearables can complement a patient's health.

As always, tailor these ideas to your expertise and the preferences of your audience. Providing valuable and actionable information will help you connect with your audience and establish yourself as a trusted source in the field.

Script for doing 60 sec Facebook or Instagram Videos

Hi, this is Dr. _____ from [NAME OF OFFICE] and today I wanted to share with you 3 tips (or secrets) for _____.

Tip #1 / Secret #1:

Tip #2 / Secret #2:

Tip #3 / Secret #3:

If you'd like to learn more about X, then we invite you to come in for a complimentary consultation at our office. Give us a call at XXX-XXX-XXXX or visit us on our website at www.website.com

ORGANIC VS PAID SOCIAL

When it comes to choosing between organic marketing and paid social media marketing, you may find yourself questioning its worth and effectiveness. We understand the importance of making an informed decision, so let's delve into the distinctions between the two to help you determine the best approach. Let's begin by exploring the differences between organic and paid social media marketing.

Organic social media refers to all of the content you post on your social media profiles without paying for promotion. This content is visible to your followers and anyone who visits your page, but it may not reach a wider audience beyond that. Organic social media is a great way to connect with your existing patients and build brand awareness and trust within your community.

There are some struggles if you decide to just use organic social media. The number of followers who actually see your posts can vary depending on several factors. Some of those factors include Facebook and Instagram algorithms, the engagement level of your followers, and the timing of your post. As a general rule, only a small percentage of your followers will see your posts on these platforms. According to some studies, organic reach on Facebook has declined to around 5.5% on average. That means if you have 100 followers, only 5 of those will actually see your posts. On Instagram, the organic reach is also estimated to be around 6% so only 6 people will see your posts out of 100 followers.

It is important to note that these numbers can vary on a variety of factors, and there are strategies you can use to increase your organic reach. You can post engaging content which we've seen usually includes personalized posts of the physician and/or the staff, or educational videos. You can also try using relevant hashtags.

Paid social media, on the other hand, involves paying to promote your content to a wider audience. This can include targeted advertisements that appear in users' feeds or sponsored posts that appear at the top of search results. Paid social media can be a powerful tool for reaching new patients and driving traffic to your website.

There are several reasons why medical offices should incorporate paid social media into their marketing strategy.

Here are just a few:

1. Expanded Reach: Paid ads allow you to extend your reach beyond your followers. By targeting specific demographics and locations, you can make sure your ads are put in front of the right people.
2. Increased Visibility: Paid ads can help you stand out from the crowd. By promoting your content, you can ensure that it appears prominently in users' feeds or search results, increasing the likelihood of engagement and conversions.
3. Faster Results: While organic social media takes time to grow and build momentum, paid ads deliver results at a quicker pace. By investing in targeted ad campaigns, you can generate immediate traffic to your website, increase appointment bookings, and achieve marketing goals faster!
4. Tracking and Analytics: Paid social media platforms provide detailed

analytics and tracking tools that allow you to measure the effectiveness of your campaigns. You can track metrics like impressions, clicks, conversions, and engagement rates, which allows you to optimize your strategy and make data-driven decisions.

While both organic and paid social media can be effective marketing strategies they serve different purposes. Organic social media is great for building relationships, sharing information, and fostering trust. Paid social media can help you reach outside of your current audience to find new potential patients and help drive traffic to your website which in turn helps with your SEO. By using both strategies together, you can create a well-rounded social media presence that will in turn help you be seen by more potential patients.

In the realm of Naturopathic Medicine marketing, social media serves as a bridge between practitioners and their communities. By strategically leveraging these platforms, NDs can not only connect with their target audience but also establish themselves as trusted authorities in complementary and alternative medicine.

I want to run paid social ads, but I don't know where to start?

Now that you've made the decision to venture into paid social media marketing, the next step is determining the right type of ad and platform to run it on. We understand that this can be overwhelming, but fear not! We're here to provide you with some valuable tips to help you navigate the world of paid ads with confidence and clarity. Let's dive in and make the most of your paid social media marketing efforts.

There are several types of paid social media ads that medical offices can run on various platforms. Here are some of the most common types:

1. Sponsored Posts: Sponsored posts are ads that appear in a user's feed and look like a regular social media post, but are labeled "sponsored". These ads can be used to promote a variety of content like events, specials, or new services.

2. Display Ads: Display ads are image-based ads that appear on the side or bottom of a user's social media feed. These ads can be used to promote a specific service or product and can include a call to action button that directs users to your website.
3. Video Ads: Video ads are similar to sponsored posts, but feature a video instead of an image. These ads can be used to showcase your medical office's services, provide educational content, give a tour of the office for potential patients, or an introduction.
4. Carousel Ads: Carousel ads allow you to showcase multiple images or videos within a single ad. This format is great for highlighting products or services offered at your office.
5. Story Ads: Story ads are full-screen ads that appear within a user's social media story. These ads can also be used to promote your services or products and can include interactive elements like polls and quizzes.

These are just a few examples of the types of paid social media ads available. Each platform offers its unique ad formats and targeting options, so it's important to choose the right type of ad for your specific marketing goals and audience.

Chapter 8

Email Marketing: Leveraging the Goldmine Within Your Practice

The Missed Opportunity of Cold Outreach

If your marketing strategy primarily revolves around SEO, Google Ads, and Facebook Ads to a cold audience, it's time to realign your focus. The low-hanging fruit lies within your practice, among your current patients. Once your foundational elements—Google My Business listing, online reputation, and social media profiles—are in place, the spotlight should shift to your existing patient base.

Nurturing the Relationships You Already Have

Your patients are not just medical records; they are potential advocates, repeat visitors and a source of valuable referrals. Start by marketing to those who have already entrusted their health to your expertise. Build upon the relationships cultivated within your practice walls and extend this rapport into the digital realm.

In an era where relationships often take root on social media, your practice's online presence is crucial. However, the challenge lies in the fact that not all your social media followers may provide you with their contact information. Moreover, the transient nature of social media platforms makes it imperative to channel these connections to a more stable and direct avenue—email.

Email serves as a bridge to traverse from online visibility to a deeper, more meaningful connection. By inviting your social media audience into the realm of your inbox, you provide them with an opportunity to truly get to know, like, and trust you. Over time, this trust transforms casual followers into committed patients, fostering repeat visits, referrals, and long-term loyalty.

The Cost-Effective Powerhouse: Email Marketing
Email marketing stands out as one of the most cost-effective and impactful ways to connect with both prospective and current patients. Doctors, in particular, boast the second-highest open rate for email marketing, surpassed only by religious organizations. The receptiveness of patients to hear from their healthcare providers creates a unique avenue for engagement and education.

Lead nurturing is the heartbeat of effective email marketing. Practices excelling at this art generate 50% more sales-ready leads at a 33% lower cost. As NDs, the potential to educate, empower, and inspire through your emails positions you as a trusted guide in your patients' health journey.

The Toolbox for Naturopathic Medicine Doctors: Popular Email Marketing Tools:

- Mailchimp: A user-friendly platform with robust features, ideal for beginners and seasoned marketers alike.

- Constant Contact: Known for its simplicity and efficient email marketing solutions, catering to diverse business needs.

- HubSpot: A comprehensive marketing and sales platform offering email marketing tools among its array of features.

- Active Campaign: Renowned for its automation capabilities, perfect for creating personalized and targeted email campaigns.

- GoHighLevel: A versatile platform providing a holistic suite of tools, including email marketing, to streamline communication and engagement.

In the realm of email marketing for naturopathic healthcare providers, a monthly newsletter emerges as a cornerstone of patient education marketing. Unlike other forms of communication, a well-crafted newsletter serves as a consistent touchpoint, keeping your practice at the forefront of your patients' minds and nurturing a relationship that transcends physical visits.

A monthly newsletter bridges the gap between appointments. It ensures that you remain a constant presence in your patients' lives, offering reassurance and valuable insights, even when they're not within your practice walls.

We all know that Naturopathic Medicine is dynamic, with advancements and insights emerging regularly. A monthly newsletter serves as your dedicated platform to educate patients on new developments, breakthroughs, and evolving practices. It's an opportunity to empower them with knowledge, fostering a sense of active participation in their well-being.

Components of an Impactful Monthly Newsletter

Leverage Health Awareness Months
Incorporate a strategic approach by aligning your newsletter with various health awareness months. Explore the comprehensive list of Health Awareness Months on medicalmarketingwhiz.com under Resources. Tailor your content to align with these themes, amplifying the relevance and resonance of your messages.

A Dash of Wellness: Healthy Recipes
One of the key components that draw engagement and anticipation is the inclusion of a healthy recipe. This not only captures attention but also elevates your newsletter's value. Patients look forward to these culinary gems, fostering a sense of well-rounded care beyond medical advice.

Celebrating Your Team
Introduce a personal touch by showcasing new staff members, celebrating work anniversaries, and acknowledging the accomplishments of your team. This not only humanizes your practice but also creates a sense of community and shared achievement.

New Treatment Options and Training Updates
Keep your patients abreast of the evolving landscape of patients's health by highlighting new treatment options, detailing relevant training you've attended, and proudly sharing any awards received. This positions your practice at the forefront of innovation and expertise.

The Power of Recognition
Include any accolades or awards your practice has earned. Patient trust is often fortified by external validation, and sharing your achievements instills confidence and pride among your audience.

Embrace the opportunity to go beyond clinical interactions, guiding your patients on a journey of holistic health. Your monthly newsletter is not just a communication tool; it's an extension of the healing touch you provide within your practice. Let it be a beacon of care, illuminating the path to wellness for every subscriber who opens their inbox to your words.

Other Ways to Use Email Marketing
While a monthly newsletter is a powerful tool, you can further leverage email marketing for a myriad of impactful engagements. Consider inviting your patients to in-office events, webinars, or workshops, fostering a sense of community and education. Promote your social media channels, encouraging subscribers to connect with your practice on various platforms for a more interactive experience. Don't shy away from seeking reviews – ask satisfied patients to share their positive experiences on Google and other review platforms, fortifying your online reputation. Share exclusive health tips, sneak peeks into upcoming treatments, or even spotlight patient success stories.

The versatility of email marketing extends beyond the routine, offering you a dynamic platform to nurture patient relationships, boost engagement, and foster a vibrant healthcare community. Email marketing is not just a strategy; it's a conduit for healing, education, and enduring connections. Embrace it, and witness the transformative impact it brings to your practice and the lives you touch.

Chapter 9

The Power of Webinars: Educate & Attract New Patients

Welcome, NDs, to a chapter dedicated to unraveling the secrets of hosting impactful webinars. In the world of naturopathic medicine, connecting with your audience is key, and webinars offer a dynamic platform to engage, educate, and empower.

Webinars allow you to reach a broad audience simultaneously, overcoming the limitations of in-person events. This is particularly valuable in health and wellness, where sensitive topics may deter attendance at physical gatherings. Addressing sensitive conditions like leaky gut, autoimmune disorders, or hormone imbalance requires a private, educational tool. Webinars offer a platform for individuals to learn from the comfort and privacy of their homes.

With the prevalence of mobile technologies, attending webinars is effortless. People can participate using smartphones, increasing accessibility and engagement.

Webinars not only drive immediate patient acquisition and new appointments but also create a lasting impact. Establishing yourself as an expert enhances branding, visibility, and future pipeline development.

Statistics show that 73 percent of marketers consider webinars an extremely effective source of high-quality leads, second only to in-person events at 77 percent. The longevity and effectiveness of webinars make them an indispensable tool.

Webinars accomplish three primary goals.
1. They provide your practice with branding and visibility within your community. Prospective patients get to know who you are, what you offer, and how you can help them. This is a crucial first step in your marketing - getting your name out there and creating awareness in your local market.

2. Second, webinars provide immediate sales and return on investment. Just like in-person events, webinars provide a path for people to make deposits and book consultations. As people learn about your new services, "meet" your staff through your virtual event videos, see results ,and hear testimonials, there are some patients who will be ready to take action right away. Be sure you have a way to collect deposits for those who "attend" because the fortune is in the follow-up.

3. Webinars also provide a lucrative future pipeline of potential new patients. Don't be discouraged if everyone who attends your webinar doesn't book an immediate appointment, because you can expect to DOUBLE or TRIPLE your conversions over time from the awareness and long-term pipeline. Every person who RSVPs is a hot lead that should be nurtured through your future social media and email marketing efforts.

Setting the Stage for a Successful Webinar

Crafting Your Webinar Topic:
Your expertise is your superpower. Begin by brainstorming some of the most common conditions or problems that your patients have questions about. What are some of the advanced treatment options that you offer that set you apart from other providers? Think about the core message you want to convey. Whether it's the latest breakthroughs in naturopathic med-

icine or essential self-care practices, make it clear, concise, and tailored to your audience's needs.

Webinar Topic Ideas:
- Transform Your Health and Sleep for Good
- Weight Management
- Gut Health
- Menopause / Hormones
- Infertility
- Autoimmune Disease
- Long Covid
- Getting to the Root of Hair Loss
- Naturopathic Approaches to Cognitive Health

Visual Appeal

Embrace visuals that resonate with your audience. Incorporate slides, infographics, and relevant images to enhance your message. Remember, a picture is worth a thousand words, and in the world of naturopathic medicine, visual clarity is paramount.

Use Google Slides, PowerPoint, Canva, or Keynote to create engaging slides with photos, videos, and infographics to help the audience better understand the content you are presenting.

Exploring Webinar Formats

Before diving into the logistics of hosting webinars, it's crucial to consider the format that suits your comfort level and effectively communicates your message. Some Naturopathic Medicine Doctors prefer the power of the PowerPoint format, utilizing slides for a show-and-tell approach. Others may find an interview-style more appealing, creating dynamic discussions with the interviewer.

Choosing the Right Streaming Platform

Now that you've envisioned your webinar, the next step is selecting the right platform for streaming. Not all platforms are created equal, and considering your goals is crucial.

Key Streaming Platforms:
- Zoom Webinar: Opt for Zoom's dedicated webinar platform, offering better control over participant engagement and eliminating distractions encountered in Zoom meetings.
- Vimeo Webinar: Explore Vimeo's new webinar platform for a reliable alternative, providing features for a seamless webinar experience.
- Webinar Jam and GoToWebinar: These platforms offer popular alternatives with specific functionalities catering to different needs.
- In-House Webinar Platform: Consider developing your own webinar platform, offering flexibility for pre-recorded sessions and live streaming on various social media channels simultaneously.

Live vs. Pre-Recorded Webinars
The decision to go live or pre-recorded is a pivotal one and depends on your goals, experience, and audience engagement preferences.

Benefits of Live Webinars:
- Real-time Interaction: Allows for immediate interaction between the presenter and the audience through features like Q&A sessions, chat, and live polls. This real-time engagement can lead to more dynamic and engaging sessions.
- Authenticity: Live webinars feel more authentic because there is no opportunity for editing or post-production. This can build trust with your audience as they know you are delivering information in real-time.
- Urgency: Live webinars create a sense of urgency, encouraging attendees to join at the scheduled time to not miss out on the live experience.

- Immediate Feedback: You can gauge the audience's reactions and understanding of the content during a live webinar. This feedback can help you adjust your presentation on the spot.

Benefits of Pre-Recorded Webinars:
- Flexibility: Pre-recorded webinars offer flexibility in terms of when and where they can be viewed. Attendees can access the content at their convenience, which can lead to a wider audience reach.
- Quality Control: Pre-recording allows you to carefully edit and fine-tune your presentation, ensuring a polished and error-free delivery. This can result in a higher-quality final product.
- Scheduling Ease: You can record the webinar at a time that's most convenient for you and your team, avoiding scheduling conflicts or technical glitches that might occur during a live event.
- Reduced Stress: Pre-recording can be less stressful for presenters, as there's no pressure to perform flawlessly in real-time. This can lead to a more relaxed and confident delivery.
- Evergreen Content: Pre-recorded webinars can be repurposed as evergreen content. They can continue to attract new viewers and generate leads long after the initial recording.

Maximizing Webinar Impact

Ideal Webinar Length and Topic Ideas:
- Keep webinar content concise, aiming for no more than 30 minutes, allowing time for Q&A.
- Consider topic ideas tailored to patients's health, such as hormonal balance, menopause, intimate health, and aesthetic treatments.

You will want to have a catchy header, information about the speaker, and the webinar topic. Don't forget your pop-up sign up form.

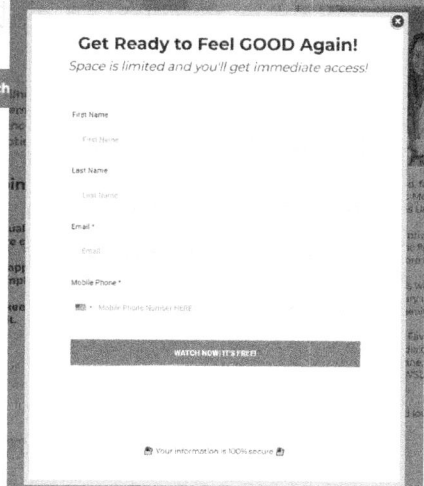

Marketing Your Webinar: Building Anticipation

Now that you've crafted an engaging webinar, it's time to ensure that the right audience is aware and excited about attending. Below are comprehensive strategies to market your webinar effectively:

1. Flyer with QR Code:
- Design an eye-catching flyer promoting your webinar and include a QR code leading directly to the registration page. Place these flyers in your office for easy access.

2. Download a Fresh Patient Email List:
- Extract a current and updated email list from your Electronic Medical Records (EMR) system. Ensure you have permission to contact patients via email.

3. Email Marketing:
- Utilize your email marketing system to send out a well-crafted email blast to your patient list. Include details about the webinar, its relevance, and the registration link.

4. Create Facebook Event Listing:
- Leverage the power of social media by creating a dedicated event listing on Facebook. Encourage followers to RSVP, share the event, and invite others.

5. Social Media Posts (FB, IG, LinkedIn):
- Regularly post updates on all your social media channels, including Facebook, Instagram, and LinkedIn. Share intriguing snippets about the webinar content, speakers, and benefits of attending.

6. Change Your Cover Photo on Facebook:
- Make your webinar prominent on Facebook by changing your cover photo to a visually appealing design with details about the upcoming event and the registration link.

7. Website (Add Registration Link on Homepage):
- Collaborate with your web developer to add a noticeable registration link on the homepage of your website. Ensure easy access for anyone visiting your site.

8. Eventbrite:
- Leverage platforms like Eventbrite to create an additional space for marketing your webinar. Eventbrite not only helps in registration but also exposes your event to a broader audience.

9. Google Business Profile:
- Optimize your Google My Business profile by updating details about your webinar. This free tool helps improve local visibility and informs potential attendees about your upcoming event.

10. Chamber of Commerce:
- Connect with your local Chamber of Commerce to feature your webinar on their website or in their communication channels. They often support local businesses and healthcare providers.

11. Press Release:
- Craft a compelling press release announcing your webinar. Distribute it to local and national media outlets, including newspapers, radio stations, and online news platforms. A well-constructed press release not only spreads the word but also contributes to your practice's search engine optimization.

By employing a mix of these marketing strategies, you can maximize the visibility of your webinar and attract a diverse audience. The goal is not only to inform but also to create anticipation and excitement around your expertise and the valuable insights you'll be sharing.

Repurposing Webinars:
- Explore repurposing your webinar as a podcast episode, expanding your reach, and elevating your authority.

- Podcast features can be promoted as an additional accolade, contributing to your status as a local expert.
- Chop up the webinar into shorter clips that you can use on social media
- Add the webinar to your YouTube channel

Congratulations, Naturopathic Medicine Doctors! You've now gained insights into the diverse formats, streaming options, and marketing strategies that can make your webinars not only informative but also powerful tools for patient education and practice growth. Get ready to take your expertise to new heights in the digital realm!

Chapter 10

Healthful Gatherings: Events & Speaking Engagements for Naturopathic Medicine

Events can be powerful revenue generators for Naturopathic Medicine Doctors, offering an effective means to quickly launch new services or discuss steps for diagnosis and treatment. Well-executed events not only boost revenue but also play a pivotal role in expanding your patient base, facilitating patient education, and fostering loyalty. To achieve these outcomes, meticulous planning and execution are crucial.

Every event should be strategically designed to:
- Welcome returning and new guests in a casual, fun, and informative setting.
- Encourage attendees to explore new services through live demos.
- Generate immediate revenue through event-exclusive pricing.
- Allow loyal patients to share testimonials.
- Provide education on new procedures, services, and products.
- Inform patients about treatment expectations.
- Recognize and thank VIPs and loyal fans.
- Create trust and differentiate your practice.

Pre-qualifiers for Success:
Prior to planning an event, ensure the following minimum requirements are met:

1. An email list of at least 1,000 contacts.
2. At least 500 Facebook or Instagram followers on your social media pages.
3. An 8-week planning period.
4. Staff commitment to promoting the event.

If you do not have these minimum requirements in place, now is the time to focus your efforts on building your email list and social media following. There's nothing worse than investing time, energy, and money into an event where no one shows up. Putting in the time to build your email list and social media first will pay off when it comes time to market your event.

Gathering Your Invite List:
Download a fresh email and mailing list from your electronic medical records. You'll want to use both email and direct mail to this list. Allow yourself time to design the mailer and get it to people's mailboxes at least 4 weeks prior to the event.

You'll also want to send at least three emails out to your entire list.

Reach out to businesses that serve a similar demographic but aren't direct competitors. For instance, consider partnering with personal trainers, yoga or pilates studios, health coaches, or nutritionists. Propose a mutually beneficial arrangement where both parties gain exposure to each other's clientele. Perhaps your event promotes overall wellness, and the partnering business can offer exclusive discounts to your attendees.

Utilize social media platforms to find and connect with local professional organizations. These groups often consist of successful patients who may be interested in attending or promoting your event.

Engage with your local Chamber of Commerce and explore opportunities to collaborate. Many local businesses, including those owned by patients, are part of the Chamber and might be interested in supporting or attending your event. Also, if you're a member of the Chamber (which you should be!) make sure to send them the invite and ask them to add it to the community calendar and email it out to all of the Chamber members.

Sales reps - Be sure to invite all of your nutriceutical sales reps and medical device sales reps to your event. They may also be able to sponsor the event with catering, educational materials, and freebies.

While a robust email list is a valuable asset, it's not the only avenue to ensure a successful in-office event. By thinking creatively and forming strategic partnerships with businesses and organizations in your community, you can expand your reach, engage with a broader audience, and make your patients's wellness event a resounding success.

Choosing the Right Timing:
Mid-week evenings (6:00 - 8:00 PM) or Saturday mornings (10:00 AM – 12:00 PM) are ideal times for events. Consider potential conflicts with local events, holidays, and other relevant matters. Ensure adequate staffing and a willingness among team members to stay late if necessary.

Also, keep in mind that your target audience is most likely busy professional people or parents. You need to give them enough advance notice for your event because they have their calendar planned out usually for several weeks (and sometimes months) at a time. This is why it's critical that you give yourself at least 6-8 weeks to really plan and market the event; 2 weeks of planning and 4 weeks of marketing!

Event Types and Themes:
Events can vary, from broad-appeal open houses to focused educational seminars. Themes add excitement and engagement.

Event Theme Ideas for Health Providers:
- Harmony in Health: A Holistic Approach to Wellness
- Serenity Soiree: Stress Relief and Mental Well-Being
- Plant-Powered Party: Discover the benefits of plant-based treatments and diets
- Autoimmune Allies: Natural Defenses for Your Health

- Long Haul Healing: Holistic Approaches to Post-COVID Care

Event Marketing Best Practices:
Marketing your event is one of the most critical steps. You need to dedicate a solid eight weeks to plan the event and get the word out. Further, be sure you are tracking all your RSVPs via phone, email, and online so that reminders and confirmations can be sent (this significantly increases the percentage of people who will attend).

Digital and Print Marketing:
Utilize both digital and print strategies. Digital methods include creating an RSVP landing page, weekly email blasts, Facebook events, live videos, website listings, Google Business postings, and Eventbrite listings. For print marketing, use color flyers placed strategically within your office and partner businesses.

Radio/Newspapers (Optional):
- Consider radio spots, press releases to local newspapers, and purchasing newspaper ads.

Personal Invitations:
- Don't rely solely on digital marketing. Ensure staff and doctors personally hand out invitations to patients. Encourage them to take flyers to the local businesses.

Wider Outreach:
- Send press releases to local newspapers and the Chamber of Commerce. Invite other business owners in your building.

Event Planning Timeline:

It's important that you give your team enough time to plan and execute the event for it to be successful. A minimum of 8 weeks should be allowed.

8 Weeks Before the Event
- ☐ Pick a season, date, and time for your event.

TIP: The best times for events are:
WINTER: Last week of January or first week of Feb
SPRING: just before Mother's Day
FALL: Last week of September, all of October, and first 2 weeks of November.

The best times are 5:30 – 7:30 pm on a weekday or a Saturday morning from 10 am-12 pm.

- [ ] Choose the event type

Examples: VIP Consult Day, Treatment-specific/Patient Pain point seminar, Broad Appeal Open House, Online Event.

TIP: Events with fun & exciting themes gain more traction! (Open House is boring!)

- [ ] Get your attendee list together

Download a fresh email list from your EMR. If you have consent, you can also do a text invite. Invitees should be encouraged to bring a friend to get an extra incentive or discount. It's also a good idea to invite salon and medical spa owners, health/fitness trainers, gym owners, and the chamber of commerce (if you are a member).

- [ ] Block your schedule on the day of the event. You should finish seeing patients early on the day of the event to make time for setting up, etc.

- [ ] Develop your event marketing materials and schedule them for distribution. Marketing materials should include the printed flyer, lobby poster, social media & web announcements, and bring-a-friend incentive images.

- [ ] Invite your sales reps if their products are included in your event promotions to help you educate and sell to attendees. Ask them to bring brochures, product samples, goodie bags, or raffle items.

☐ Secure people for demos and patient testimonials.

TIP: Showing a live demo at your event or giving lab testing will SIGNIFICANTLY increase your sales at the event. Also, keep in mind that prospective patients also want to hear from people who have worked with you, so consider asking a patient to give a testimonial.

☐ Plan your food/drinks.

TIP: Do not go overboard with food & drinks. People tend not to eat a lot at these events so simple is better! Veggie Tray, Fruit & Cheese tray, and mini desserts are ideal. Serve small bottles of water, tea, or a nice beverage dispenser with fruit for drinks. Some offices like to offer wine or mimosas too. Costco or Sam's Club are great options to purchase your supplies.

☐ If you aren't already enrolled, sign up for a Cherry payment plan to offer to attendees at the event.

Sign up for Cherry here >>

4-6 Weeks Before the Event

☐ Launch your event marketing

PRINT MATERIALS: Event flyers should be posted in the waiting room, all treatment rooms, bathrooms, the elevator, and check-in/check-out areas. Staff should be handing out invitations to everyone who visits the office. TIP: Do not assume that people will see the flyers posted. It is critical to personally hand invites to everyone who comes into the office either at check-in or check-out. Bring flyers to neighboring businesses.

EMAIL BLASTS should be sent weekly 4 weeks prior to the event through the week of the event. The e-blasts should include the digital image of the event flyer and a link to RSVP online. TIP: Tuesdays at 10:00 AM is the best time to send out the weekly email invites.

POST the event details and images on Facebook, Instagram, Google My Business, and Eventbrite.

☐ RSVP Management

TIP: Be sure your staff is trained to collect RSVPs by phone and ask for name, phone & email address for confirmation. Use an RSVP tally sheet at the reception desk to make it easy for staff to track the RSVP that come in by phone. Be sure your staff knows how to answer questions about the event. Monitor your RSVP weekly and be sure to contact each RSVP to let them know they are confirmed. Don't wait until the week before to confirm the RSVPs.

☐ Order items for goodie bags (product samples, small chocolates, discount coupons)

☐ Check the inventory of any products you may be selling on the event day. Place any orders if necessary to ensure you have enough stock.

☐ Prepare your event presentation slides.

TIP: The presentation should be no longer than 20-25 minutes followed by a 10 min Q&A and patient testimonial.

☐ Have staff sign up for their roles at the event.

Event Roles for Staff

EVENT SET UP (3):
JOB: Assist with set up of the event.

RSVP CONTACT:
JOB: Collect RSVPs pre-event. Keep track of Name, Email & Phone number for all RSVPs. Contact each person prior to the event to confirm their attendance.

CHECK-IN FOR EVENT:
JOB: Greet guests as they arrive. Check them off of the RSVP list and give them their Goodie Bags & Pricing menu before showing them into the reception area.

DRINK STATION (2):
JOB: Greet incoming guests with a refreshment.

FOOD STATION/REPLENISHER:
JOB: Watch food levels, keep food / refreshments stocked throughout the event.

DEVICE Q & A:
JOB: Handle all device questions - offer to book consultation if there is an interest.

PROCEDURE Q & A:
JOB: Handle all procedure questions - offer to book consultation if there is an interest.

SOCIALIZERS:
JOB: Help to guide people from the check in area into the different stations, make conversation, etc. - Very important at the beginning of the event before the flow is obvious and there is a crowd.

PHOTO/VIDEO:
JOB: Take photos and short videos during the event. This person should have a good quality phone. Take the photos and videos (hold phone horizontal) and be sure to keep track of names of who is photographed for Facebook tagging, etc. post event.

CLEAN UP (3):
JOB: Assist with event tear down

2 Weeks Before The Event

- [ ] Check the number of RSVPs on the RSVP tally sheet, online registration, Eventbrite, and Facebook.

TIP: Plan for a 60% attendance rate of those who RSVP'd. If you need more attendance, consider running a Facebook ad for the event. Also, have a backup plan if you are overbooked (add overflow event day).

- [ ] Reconfirm with reps, live demo patients, and testimonials.

- [ ] Develop & print signage for each station (device demos, procedures, treatments, etc.), raffle tickets, and navigational signs for the event.

- [ ] Develop a checkout with all promotions listed so that attendees can easily check packages they are interested in purchasing a package or putting down a deposit.

- [ ] Make sure you have all audio/visual equipment necessary (laptop, TV or projector, screen, HDMI cord, speaker)

1 Week Before The Event

- [ ] Reconfirm date for all deliveries

- [ ] Practice your PowerPoint presentation.

- [ ] If you have a call-in day for your event for those who cannot attend but still want to take advantage of the event only specials, make sure you're staffed and ready to handle the call volume.

- [ ] Contact all RSVPs to remind them about the event. This includes phone RSVP, online registration, Eventbrite, and Facebook. Encourage each person to bring a friend for an extra discount or free service. Facebook "Interested" and "Going" should be messaged through Facebook and look them up in your system to see if you have a phone number on file, so you can call them to remind them about the event.

Event Day

- [ ] Event set-up: Check-in table and goodie bag distribution, check-out area, demo areas, treatment rooms/stations should each have a raffle bowl which encourages attendees to visit each station, food table, drink table/Bar. Arrange seating to ensure all guests can see the presentation. Place handouts or questionnaires on each seat.

- [ ] Review each staff member's responsibility from the event staff signup sheet.

- [ ] Set up audio/visual and test it to ensure speakers are working, videos play, etc.

- [ ] Have Cherry Financing information available.

- [ ] During the event have staff observe and take notes on interests or concerns expressed by guests for use in consultations or in customizing follow-up calls.

☐ Once your presentation is complete, let your guests know that staff is available to schedule appointments and take deposits for the event-only pricing. Make sure you have multiple members of your staff available to take deposits/payments in order to reduce wait time.

Event Follow Up

Use this time as an opportunity to stay in contact with the attendees. These strategies will help your practice maximize the return on investment from your event.

☐ Send "Thank You" emails or personal notes to attendees.

☐ Contact each booked patient to set an appointment (if not done at the event itself).

☐ Contact any no-shows to invite back for a free consult after the event special.

☐ Create a video from the event and post it on social media thanking those who attended. Remind everyone about the event pricing and set a deadline by which the offer will expire.

Hosting well-planned and strategically executed in-office events can be a game-changer for naturopathic medicine practices. These events offer a unique opportunity to welcome both new and returning guests, foster genuine connections, and generate immediate revenue through exclusive offerings. By adhering to pre-qualifiers and dedicating time to build your email list and social media following, you lay the groundwork for a successful event. Whether it's a broad-appeal open house, a focused educational seminar, or a themed gathering, events contribute to growing your patient base, providing valuable education, and fostering lasting relationships with your community. The key is meticulous planning, thoughtful marketing, and a commitment to making each event a memorable and beneficial experience for both your practice and your attendees.

Unlocking Opportunities through Speaking Engagements: Connecting with Your Audience Beyond the Office

When it comes to expanding your reach and establishing authority in your field, speaking engagements offer a powerful avenue for engagement. Instead of hosting an event at your office, consider taking your expertise directly to the audience by participating in various speaking opportunities. Below are strategies to leverage speaking engagements for maximum impact:

Identify and Reach Out to Local patients's Groups:

Country Clubs: Many country clubs host events and luncheons where guest speakers are welcome. Reach out to the event organizers, offering to share valuable insights on health and wellness. This platform allows you to connect with an audience already invested in their well-being.

Business Owner Groups: Connect with local business owner groups or associations. Offer to speak at their meetings, providing information on patients's health topics relevant to their members. This not only positions you as an expert but also opens doors for potential collaborations.

Wellness Events: Cities host wellness events for the community. Inquire about opportunities to be a featured speaker, addressing topics that resonate with the audience. This can include anything from mental health to longevity medicine.

Utilize Professional Networks: Healthcare Conferences and Seminars: Explore opportunities to speak at healthcare conferences or seminars. Sharing your expertise with fellow healthcare professionals not only establishes credibility but also fosters referrals and collaborations.

Community Health Fairs: Participate in community health fairs where you can offer informative talks on whole body health. Engaging with the community in this way builds trust and positions your practice as a resource for healthcare needs.

Craft Compelling Presentation Topics: Tailor Topics to Your Audience: When proposing speaking engagements, customize your presentation topics to cater to the specific interests and concerns of the audience. This could range from gut health or to stress management techniques for busy professionals.

Interactive Workshops: Consider hosting interactive workshops or Q&A sessions to actively engage the audience. This format not only imparts valuable information but also fosters a connection between you and your audience.

Collaborate with Influencers: Partner with influencers or online personalities in the health and wellness space to co-host virtual events. This collaboration can introduce your expertise to a new and engaged audience.

Speaking engagements provide a dynamic platform to share your expertise, connect with diverse audiences, and establish your practice as a trusted resource. By strategically targeting different groups and events, you can extend your influence, build meaningful connections, and ultimately attract new patients to your practice.

Chapter 11

Podcasting for Naturopathic Medicine Doctors: Amplifying Influence Beyond the Microphone

The influence of successful healthcare podcasts extends beyond the immediate listener base, serving as platforms for change and influencing healthcare practices and patient experiences. For Naturopathic Medicine Doctors, the power of podcasts goes beyond individual stories—they shape public discourse, influence policy, and highlight the importance of preventative medicine voices in driving the healthcare conversation forward.

Podcast listeners, including a significant portion of women, represent a diverse demographic profile that spans various education and income levels. Research indicates that podcast audiences tend to have higher education levels, with a substantial portion having completed college or attained advanced degrees. Similarly, podcast consumers often fall within higher income brackets, reflecting a demographic that is economically well-positioned. This trend is particularly noteworthy among female listeners, highlighting an engaged and educated audience. The appeal of podcasts to this demographic can be attributed to the on-demand nature of the medium, allowing patients to access content that aligns with their interests, professional pursuits, and personal growth at their convenience. As the podcasting landscape continues to evolve, understanding and catering to the diverse demographics of listeners will remain essential for content creators and marketers alike.

Podcasting as a Marketing Tool: Understanding the Role

Podcasting offers a unique opportunity to share thought leadership, valuable insights, and build meaningful connections with the audience. Podcasting's blend of storytelling and information sharing is particularly well-suited for the complex and personal nature of healthcare.

Reach and trust form the twin pillars of effective marketing, and podcasting enhances both. By consistently providing valuable content, you can extend your influence beyond local communities to a global audience. The intimacy of audio allows for one-on-one connections, creating a sense of trust that's often challenging to achieve through other mediums.

Being featured on a podcast or hosting one can significantly elevate your perceived expertise and credibility. Imagine a prospective patient visiting a website and discovering that their healthcare provider has been a guest on a podcast or, even more impressively, hosts their own show. This not only communicates a commitment to staying at the forefront of their field but also reflects a dedication to patient education and well-being.

The podcast medium, with its intimate and conversational nature, provides an opportunity for healthcare professionals to share valuable insights, discuss advancements in their specialty, and connect with a broader audience. For the patient, this presence on a podcast platform signals that the doctor is not only knowledgeable but also actively engaged in disseminating information to improve patients's lives. The association with podcasting, as both a guest and a host, creates a powerful narrative of expertise, authority, and a genuine passion for patient care.

Integrating Podcasting into Your Marketing Strategy

Podcasting shouldn't exist in isolation but as an integral part of a multifaceted marketing strategy. Aligning podcast content with the practice's goals and messaging ensures a cohesive experience for patients and listeners. By promoting the podcast through social media, newsletters, and the practice's website, providers create a harmonious extension of their overall brand.

Embarking on a podcasting journey can be both exciting and daunting, so a good first step is to try and find an existing podcast show that has an established audience and get on their show as a guest expert. Being a guest on someone else's show serves as a stepping stone, offering insights into the podcasting world before taking the plunge into hosting your own. This not only provides a valuable learning experience but also introduces you to an established audience. Leveraging existing podcasts allows you to grasp the dynamics of the medium, understand audience expectations, and refine your communication style. It's a collaborative entry point that not only builds confidence but also lays the foundation for creating meaningful connections within the podcasting community.

Finding the Right Podcast and Making Your Pitch

Researching Podcasts with a Naturopathic Medicine-Centric Audience

Before diving into the podcasting world, it's essential to identify shows that align with your target audience. Start your research by leveraging online platforms and directories dedicated to podcasts. Websites like Apple Podcasts, Spotify, or even niche podcast directories can be valuable resources. Consider these steps:

> Use Podcast Directories: Explore podcast platforms and directories to find shows that cater to topics relevant to wellness, holistic health, or nutrition. Look for podcasts with engaged audiences and a format that resonates with you.
>
> Review Ratings and Reviews: Check the ratings and reviews of potential podcasts. Positive reviews often indicate an engaged and supportive audience, making it an ideal platform to share your expertise.
>
> Utilize Social Media: Platforms like Twitter, LinkedIn, and Facebook are excellent for connecting with podcasters. Join relevant

groups or follow hashtags related to natural health podcasts. Many podcasters announce guest opportunities on these platforms.

Collaborate with Influencers: Patient influencers in healthcare or wellness often collaborate with podcasts. Identify influencers in your field and see if they've been featured on any podcasts. This can be a good starting point for finding shows that resonate with your target audience.

Crafting a Compelling Pitch

Once you've identified potential podcasts, the next step is reaching out to podcasters. Here's a guide on how to create an engaging pitch:

Introduction: Start with a concise introduction. Mention your name, your expertise, and express genuine admiration for their podcast.

Relevance: Explain why your expertise aligns with their podcast's themes and audience. Highlight specific topics you can discuss that would provide value to their listeners.

Credentials: Showcase your credentials briefly. Mention any notable awards, affiliations, or certifications that establish your authority in the field.

Benefits: Clearly outline the benefits of having you as a guest. Emphasize how your insights can contribute to their audience's knowledge and well-being.

Engagement: Express your commitment to actively engage with your audience. This could involve promoting the episode on your social channels, participating in post-release discussions, or offering additional resources.

Previous Experience: If you've been featured on other podcasts or media outlets, share these experiences. It adds credibility to your pitch.

Contact Information: Provide clear and easily accessible contact information. Make it easy for the podcaster to follow up with you.

Example Podcast Outreach Email:

Subject: Podcast Guest?

Hey {{contact_name}},

I wanted to check to see if you are in charge of booking guests on {{contact_company||your podcast}}.

Are you open to a guest slot / interview on your podcast in the next month or so?

If so, I'd love to have Dr. Jane Doe, licensed naturopathic doctor, come on and do an episode. I have a few ideas for topics relevant to your audience, including:

[insert topics here]

Here's a real quick overview of why she would be a great fit for your audience and your podcast...

[insert experience here]

Let me know what you think.

Happy to answer any questions you may have and look forward to meeting you!

Here to help,
{{your podcast manager's name}}

Launching Your Own Podcast

Embarking on your podcasting journey is an exciting venture, and with the simplicity offered by Spotify for Podcasters, it's never been easier to share your insights and expertise with a global audience. Spotify for Podcasters serves as a user-friendly hub, providing an accessible entry point for both novice and seasoned podcasters alike. The platform not only hosts your podcast content on Spotify but also streamlines the process of syndicating your episodes across various popular platforms, including Apple Podcasts, I Heart Radio, Google Podcasts, Tuner, and more. This all-in-one functionality simplifies the complexities of podcast distribution, making it an ideal starting point for those looking to maximize their reach without delving into the intricacies of each individual platform.

Whether you're a Naturopathic Doctor eager to educate your audience or an enthusiast wanting to delve into meaningful conversations, Spotify for Podcasters offers a seamless and efficient solution to help you make your mark in the podcasting realm.

Let's explore how you can harness the power of Spotify for Podcasters to launch your own podcast and extend your influence across diverse podcasting platforms.

Here's a straightforward guide to help you get started:
Setting up your Spotify for Podcasters account is a straightforward process that puts you in control of sharing your content with a broad audience. Here's a step-by-step guide to help you get started:

1. Create a Spotify Account:
If you don't already have one, start by creating a Spotify account. You can sign up on the Spotify for Podcasters website.

2. Log In to Spotify for Podcasters:
Once you have a Spotify account, log in to Spotify for Podcasters using your Spotify credentials. You can access the Spotify for Podcasters dashboard on the official website.

3. Claim Your Podcast:

If you've already published your podcast on a hosting platform, you can claim it on Spotify for Podcasters. Enter your podcast's RSS feed URL during the claiming process. If your podcast is not yet published, you can submit it directly to Spotify.

4. Verify Your Ownership:

Spotify will guide you through a verification process to confirm that you own the podcast. This typically involves responding to an email sent to your podcast's official email address or adding a unique code to your podcast description.

5. Customize Your Podcast Profile:

Once ownership is verified, you can customize your podcast profile. This includes adding a profile image, description, and other relevant details. Make sure to create a compelling profile that accurately represents your podcast. Design eye-catching podcast artwork that reflects your brand. Ensure it meets the specifications of various podcast platforms.

Planning Your Podcast

> Define the purpose, format, and target audience for your podcast. Outline your initial episodes and create engaging content that aligns with your expertise and resonates with your audience.
>
> Educational Deep Dives:
> Create episodes that focus on in-depth discussions about specific disease states, treatment options, or medical procedures. Break down complex medical topics in a way that is accessible to a general audience, providing valuable insights into patients' health issues.
>
> Expert Interviews:
> Invite expert guests to share their expertise on various patients's health topics. Conduct interviews to delve into specific areas of interest, allowing listeners to benefit from diverse perspectives and insights.

Patient Success Stories:
Share inspiring stories from patients who have experienced positive outcomes through your care. Discuss their journeys, high lighting the impact your medical expertise has had on their lives. This format can humanize healthcare and offer hope to others.

Advancements in Holistic Health:
Stay at the forefront of naturopathic medicine advancements by discussing the latest breakthroughs, research findings, and techno logical innovations in holistic health. Keep your audience in formed about emerging trends and how they may impact health care.

Myths and FAQs:
Address common misconceptions or myths related to health care. Take the time to answer frequently asked questions, proving evidence-based information to dispel myths and empower your audience with accurate knowledge.

Preventive Care Talks:
Focus on preventive care by discussing lifestyle choices, wellness strategies, and proactive approaches to maintaining patients' health. Provide practical tips for preventing common health issues and promoting overall well-being.

Case Studies:
Present real-life case studies to illustrate diagnostic challenges, treatment plans, and successful outcomes. Use anonymized cases to educate your audience about the complexities of various health issues.

Mind-Body Connection:
Explore the interconnectedness of mental and physical health. Discuss topics related to stress management, mental well-being, and their impact on patients's health. Consider inviting mental health professionals to contribute to these discussions.

Holistic Health Talks:
Take a holistic approach to patients's health by discussing complementary and alternative therapies, nutrition, and lifestyle factors that contribute to overall well-being. Offer a well-rounded perspective on health and wellness.

By incorporating a variety of podcast formats, NDs can engage their audience with diverse and valuable content, catering to different interests and preferences within the broader healthcare landscape.

Record Your Episodes
Use your laptop or smartphone to record your podcast episodes. Ensure a quiet recording environment, and make use of your chosen microphone for optimal sound quality.

Edit Your Episodes
Edit your recordings to enhance audio quality and eliminate any unnecessary elements. Free software like Audacity or GarageBand can be great starting points for editing.

Submit Episodes:
After claiming your podcast, and recording your episodes, you can submit the episodes for consideration. Spotify will review the content to ensure it complies with their guidelines. Once approved, your episodes will be available on the Spotify platform.

Utilize Spotify for Podcasters Dashboard:
Explore the Spotify for Podcasters dashboard, where you can track various statistics and insights about your podcast. This includes listener demographics, episode performance, and more.

Syndicate to Other Platforms:
One of the key advantages of Spotify for Podcasters is the ability to syndicate your podcast to other popular platforms. In the dashboard, you'll find options to distribute your content to platforms like Apple Podcasts, Google Podcasts, and more.

Techniques for Growing Your Podcast Listenership

Growing a podcast's listenership is a strategic endeavor critical for amplifying its reach and deepening its impact. A broader audience not only translates into greater influence but also ensures that the valuable insights shared are disseminated widely, particularly to those who stand to benefit most. For healthcare podcasts, especially those offering a female perspective, cultivating a dedicated following is key to becoming a trusted resource in the field.

Let's look at some popular techniques.

Expanding Reach Through Strategic Guest Selection:

Inviting guests to your podcast can have a multiplicative effect on your listenership. When choosing guests, look for individuals with their own following who can bring new audiences to your show. This could include other healthcare professionals, patient advocates, or influencers within the wellness space. The cross-pollination of audiences can lead to a substantial increase in your listener base.

Utilizing SEO for Discoverability:

Optimizing your podcast for search engines is a powerful way to attract new listeners. This involves using relevant keywords in your episode titles, descriptions, and show notes. Conduct keyword research to understand what your target audience is searching for and incorporate these terms naturally into your content. SEO practices can vastly improve your podcast's visibility on platforms and search engines, drawing in a crowd actively seeking healthcare information.

Engagement-Driven Content:

Audience engagement is a driving force in expanding listenership. Create content that invites interaction, such as Q&A sessions, listener polls, or episodes that address listener-submitted stories and questions. Engagement not only fosters a community around your podcast but also encourages sharing, which can organically grow your audience.

Consistency in Publishing:

Maintaining a consistent publishing schedule builds listener habits and expectations. Whether it's weekly, bi-weekly, or monthly, a regular cadence keeps your audience coming back for more and can lead to higher engagement rates and sharing among listeners.

Listener Retention Strategies:
While attracting new listeners is crucial, retaining them is equally important. This can be achieved by ensuring high-quality content in every episode, providing a mix of evergreen and timely topics, and creating a narrative arc or thematic continuity that compels listeners to return.

Community Building:
Foster a sense of community around your podcast by encouraging listeners to connect with you and each other. This could be facilitated through online forums, social media groups, or live events. A strong community not only supports listener retention but also serves as a foundation for word-of-mouth growth.

Partnerships and Collaborations:
Forming partnerships with other podcasts, healthcare organizations, or community groups can introduce your podcast to wider audiences. Look for collaboration opportunities where you can offer value to the partner's audience, such as guest exchanges, shared content, or joint events.

Advertising and Promotions:
Invest in advertising your podcast on platforms where potential listeners spend their time. Consider promotions on other podcasts, social media ads, and targeted campaigns on healthcare-related websites and forums.

Leveraging Social Media Platforms:
Social media is an invaluable tool for podcast growth. Share each episode across all your channels, use engaging visuals or audiograms to capture attention, and tag your guests and relevant influencers to extend your reach. Regularly interact with your followers, and use social media to tease upcoming episodes, share behind-the-scenes content, and celebrate milestones, all of which can boost listener investment and growth.

Social media platforms are indispensable tools for amplifying your podcast's reach. By creating engaging content that can be shared across these platforms, you can tap into a vast audience who may not have discovered your podcast otherwise.

Techniques include:
- Snippet Sharing: Share short, captivating audio or video snippets from your episodes that can pique interest and spark conversations.
- Hashtag Usage: Utilize trending and relevant hashtags to increase the visibility of your posts to those interested in healthcare topics.
- Interactive Content: Create polls, Q&As, and other interactive content on social media to engage with your audience and encourage them to check out the podcast.
- Cross-promotion with other podcasters or influencers in the healthcare space can also be invaluable. By mentioning each other's content or even guesting on each other's shows, you can cross-pollinate your audiences and grow together.

Networking is a powerful strategy for growth. It involves:

Collaborative Episodes: Invite other healthcare professionals to share their expertise on your podcast. This not only enriches your content but also allows you to reach the guest's audience.

Professional Conferences and Events: Attend healthcare events and conferences to meet potential guests and listeners who have a vested interest in your content.

Podcasting Communities: Join podcasting groups and forums to exchange tips with fellow podcasters, find collaboration opportunities, and learn from others' experiences.

By implementing these techniques, your podcast can gradually build a robust and dedicated listenership. Engagement on social media, strategic cross-promotion, and active networking are key to establishing your podcast as a go-to resource within the healthcare community.

Monitor Analytics:

Keep track of your podcast's performance through the analytics provided on the Spotify for Podcasters dashboard. This data will help you understand your audience better and refine your content strategy.

Launching a podcast may seem intricate initially, but with these simple steps, you'll be well on your way to sharing your expertise with a global audience. Don't forget to enjoy the process and embrace the learning curve as you become more comfortable with the art of podcasting.

Chapter 12

Promotional Calendar of Ideas for Naturopathic Medicine Doctors

Monthly themes and seasonal promotions help provide fresh content for social media posts, press releases, or fresh content for your website. Use the following list to help brainstorm and plan your calendar for the year.

January: *Plan in November, promote in December*
Plan for the year with your patients; make an annual treatment plan together every January. Offer sweet treats like hot chocolate to make a warmer reception on chilly days.
- New Year, New You
- Sticking to your resolutions
- National Staying Healthy Month
- National Thank You Month

February: *Plan in December, promote in January*
Tip: Give patients each a rose the week of Valentine's Day
- National Heart Health Month
- Superbowl party for patients
- Groundhog Day - don't let your health get stuck in a rut
- Marti Gras
- Grammy Awards

- The Oscars
- Valentine's Day / Galentines Day

March: *Plan in January, promote in February*
With spring break in full swing and summer just around the corner, this is the time for patients to start getting summer-ready.
- Sleep Awareness Week (1st week of March)
- Doctor's Day - March 30
- Daylight Savings - Spring Forward
- March Madness
- March 17: St Patrick's Day
- Pi Day 3.14
- National Nutrition Month

April: *Plan in February, promote in March*
Considering a new promotional item? Give patients branded umbrellas to protect them from April showers.
- April 1: April Fools Day
- April 15 - Tax Day
- April 22 - Earth Day
- Infertility Awareness Week (3rd week of April)
- Administrative Professionals Day (Wednesday of the Last Full Week in April)

May: *Plan in March, promote in April*
Consider a special gift for teachers or nurses or a way to reach this group and say thank you with a gift from the practice.
- May 6: National Nurses Day
- May 8: National Teacher's Day
- May 12: Nurses Day
- National patients's Health Week
- Military Spouses Day - day before Mother's Day
- Mother's Day - Mother/Daughter appointments
- Skin Cancer Awareness Month - SPF
- Osteoporosis Awareness Month
- Food Allergy Month

- Women's Health Week (2nd week of May)
- Getting Ready for Summer
- Memorial Day
- Self-Love Month

June: Plan in April, promote in May
National Best Friend's Day is a great time to run a promotion that encourages patients to spread the word to their friends.
- Acne Awareness Month
- Men's Health Month
- June 8: Best Friend's Day
- June 15: The Power of a Smile Day
- Father's Day
- National Rose Month

July: *Plan in May, promote in June*
With travel being on everyone's mind, consider unique ways to keep patients engaged through their busy summer months.
- July 4: Independence Day
- July 31: National Parents Day
- Fibroid Awareness Month

August: *Plan in June, promote in July*
This time of year is great to encourage patients to treat themselves to healthy living.
- August 1: National Girlfriend's Day
- National Relaxation Day
- National Smile Week
- Psoriasis Awareness Month
- National Women's Day
- National Relaxation Day
- National Couples Day
- National Senior Citizens Day
- Women's Equality Day
- National Dog Day

- National Red Wine Day
- National Heroes Day

September: *Plan in July, promote in August*
This is the time when kids are back in school and moms can focus on themselves again. Offer apple cider as a free refreshment at the office.
- Healthy Aging Month
- Menopause Awareness Month
- Grandparents Day (first Sunday after Labor Day)
- Ovarian Cancer Awareness Month
- PCOS (Polycystic Ovarian Syndrome) Month

October: *Plan in August, promote in September*
Halloween, Sweetest Day, and Breast Cancer are perfect promotions for October. Consider donating $ to Breast Cancer research this month.
- Halloween
- National Popcorn Month
- National Physician Assistants Week (2nd week of Oct)
- Oct 16: National Bosses Day
- Oct 20: Sweetest Day
- Breast Cancer Prevention Month (wear pink!)

November: *Plan in September, promote in October*
Put out a Santa Wish list that patients can fill out for health gifts - mail the lists to their significant other for them!
- Thankful Thursdays
- Black Friday & Cyber Monday specials
- National Healthy Skin Month
- National Diabetes Awareness Month
- Bladder Health Month
- Fall Back - Daylight Savings time ends
- Getting ready for holiday events

December: *Plan in October, promote in November*
Send out holiday cards to your patients with a $25-50 gift certificate included for services and include a second card they can give to a friend.

Holiday card promotions can help make your January very busy!
- Give the gift of wellness
- Gift card for a friend option
- Holiday cards with $50 gift certificates
- Stocking stuffers, gift cards
- Gift for a year - whole year package
- 12 Days of Christmas

Conclusion

Your Journey to Becoming the #1 Naturopathic Medicine Doctor

Congratulations! You've embarked on a transformative journey, delving into the intricate realm of marketing tailored specifically for NDs. As we bring our comprehensive guide to a close, let's reflect on the key insights and strategies that will propel you toward becoming the unrivaled #1 Naturopathic Medicine Doctor in your community.

Embracing the Power of Strategic Marketing
In the dynamic landscape of healthcare, strategic marketing is your compass, guiding you through the intricacies of patient engagement, digital presence, and community outreach. By unveiling the foundations of successful ND marketing (Chapter 1) and transforming your approach (Chapter 2), you've laid the groundwork for a robust strategy that resonates with your audience.

Understanding and Connecting with Your Ideal Patient
Central to your success is the ability to understand and connect with your ideal patient. Chapter 3 has equipped you with the tools to decipher the factors influencing patients' choices. By aligning your services with their needs, you not only attract but retain a loyal patient base.
Establishing Authority in Naturopathic Medicine

Your website serves as the virtual face of your practice (Chapter 4). Position yourself as the authority in naturopathic medicine, providing a wealth of information that educates and empowers your audience. A strong online presence, coupled with local SEO strategies (Chapter 5), ensures that your practice is easily discoverable.

Building Trust through Reviews and Social Media Mastery

Trust is the cornerstone of patient-doctor relationships. Chapter 6 emphasized the power of Google reviews in building credibility and boosting SEO. Meanwhile, in Chapter 7, you mastered social media, using it not only as a platform for education but also as a tool for effective advertising. By leveraging these digital channels, you've connected with patients in ways that transcend the traditional doctor-patient dynamic.

Unlocking the Potential of Email Marketing and Webinars

Email marketing (Chapter 8) has allowed you to tap into the goldmine within your practice, fostering ongoing communication with your patients. Webinars (Chapter 9) have become a powerful educational tool, positioning you as a thought leader and attracting new patients seeking your expertise.

Nurturing Relationships Through In-Office Events and Podcasting

Local engagement is vital, and Chapter 10 illustrated how healthful gatherings can solidify your presence in the community. Podcasting (Chapter 11) has amplified your influence beyond the confines of your office, reaching a broader audience and establishing you as a trusted voice in health and wellness.

Crafting a Promotional Calendar for Lasting Impact

Chapter 12 provided you with a roadmap for orchestrating a promotional calendar. By aligning your marketing efforts with key events and themes, you've created a rhythm that resonates with your audience, keeping your practice top-of-mind throughout the year.

A Journey, Not a Destination

As we conclude this guide, remember that your journey to becoming the

#1 Naturopathic Medicine Doctor is ongoing. The strategies outlined here are not static; they evolve with the ever-changing landscape of healthcare and patient expectations. Continue to adapt, innovate, and embrace new opportunities that arise.

Your Impact Goes Beyond Medicine
In your pursuit of excellence, recognize that your impact extends beyond health care. You are not just a provider; you are a beacon of health and wellness in the lives of your patients. Your commitment to education, community engagement, and patient-centric care distinguishes you as a leader in your community.

The Future is Yours
Armed with the knowledge and tools presented in this guide, the future is yours to shape. Embrace the challenges, celebrate the victories, and remember that your dedication to naturopathic medicine is a force that transcends the confines of your practice. As you navigate this journey, may you continue to inspire, educate, and, above all, make a lasting impact on the well-being of the patients you serve.

Make sure to subscribe to our Podcast "Lady Doc Marketing"
The 'Lady Doc Marketing,' podcast is dedicated to empowering female health providers with the tools, confidence, and community needed to supercharge their marketing efforts and elevate their practices. Our show delves into all of the taboo topics centered around the unique challenges and opportunities that come with marketing in the female health field. Each episode is packed with actionable tips, insightful interviews, and a hefty dose of empowerment to help you navigate the world of marketing with ease and flair. Subscribe now to transform your practice and empower your journey!

Scan the QR code to listen now

BOOK YOUR STRATAGY CALL WITH
Lori Werner

Founder of Medical Marketing Whiz

If you're in the healthcare industry and looking to take your business to the next level, booking a strategy call with the founder of Medical Marketing Whiz, is a game-changer you can't afford to miss. With her wealth of experience and expertise in medical marketing, Lori has helped numerous healthcare professionals achieve growth and success. During a strategy call with Lori, you will gain valuable insights tailored specifically to your practice, unlocking strategies to attract more patients, increase revenue, and enhance your online presence. Don't miss this opportunity to tap into our proven methods and propel your healthcare practice into the #1 office in your area.

Scan the QR code to book your strategy call

or visit:
https://medmarketingwhiz.com/ladydocs-call

Special Bonuses for Lady Docs Marketing Readers!

As a token of our appreciation for choosing "Lady Doc Marketing" as your guide to success, we're excited to offer not one, but two exclusive bonuses: Access to our Medical Marketing Whiz Masterclass and a month FREE of our Dr. Marketing Toolkit.

1. **Medical Marketing Whiz Masterclass:** Secure your complimentary seat at the Medical Marketing Whiz masterclass on "The 4 Essential Pillars of Medical Marketing." To register for this enlightening webinar, visit ***https://medmarketingwhiz.com/book***. Gain deeper insights into the strategies outlined in your Lady Doc Marketing book and take your practice to new heights.

   Scan the QR code to register

THE DR. MARKETING TOOLKIT

Unlock the Power of DIY Marketing for Doctors

The Dr. Marketing Toolkit is so simple, comprehensive, and effective that you can turn any staff member into a confident marketer within weeks.

1. **Dr. Marketing Toolkit Access:** We're also thrilled to provide you with free access to the DR. MARKETING TOOLKIT – the ultimate do-it-yourself program tailored for doctors like you. This comprehensive toolkit is designed to turn any staff member into a confident marketer within weeks. Here's what you can expect:

A Wealth of Marketing Tools & Training: Inside the Dr. Marketing Toolkit, discover a treasure trove of invaluable resources. From insightful training videos to ready-to-use Canva templates, email marketing templates, and webinar PowerPoint slide decks – we've got you covered.

Save Time and Effort: The Dr. Marketing Toolkit eliminates the hassle of searching through endless files. Your staff members can conveniently access everything they need in one centralized hub. With just a few clicks, they can watch training videos, download social media tools, launch your email newsletter, and plan your next webinar – saving you valuable time and effort.

Instant 24/7 Access to $43,925 Worth of Resources: Get free access by entering code **LADYDOC** at checkout for 1 month free. (Cancel anytime, no strings attached).

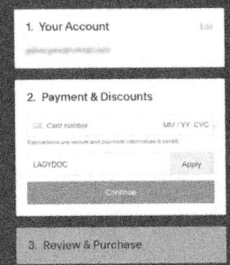

To claim your bonuses and propel your practice to new heights, register for the FREE masterclass at *https://medmarketingwhiz.com/book* and access the Dr. Marketing Toolkit *www.drmarketingtoolkit.com* using the code **LADYDOC** at checkout. Thank you for choosing Lady Docs Marketing – we're here to support your journey to success!

Stay tuned for more Marketing Guides and Resources from Medical Marketing Whiz

Make sure to follow us on Facebook and Instagram for real time updates.

@medicalmarketingwhiz

Client Testimonials

"Lori Werner's marketing knowledge is incredible. Lori knows every platform to help with visibility and marketing my business. She is full of easy accomplishable ideas/tasks to help bring more awareness to my business and bring more patients and revenue. I highly recommend."
~ *Suny Caminero, MD*

"Lori and Sherry at Medical Marketing Whiz are simply the best. Not only do they make marketing my practice much easier, but they also have taught me how to grow my brand. While they have been working with me, my organic instagram followers have increased by 50%. They make it easy for us to stay on top of marketing. I would highly recommend them!"
~ *Danielle DeLuca-Pytell*

"Lori's team at Medical Marketing Whiz has provided us with advice and leadership assisting our practice with marketing strategies that have helped our practice grow. The teams help and guidance is well worth the cost. I highly recommend them."
~ *Lon Katz*

"Just started working with Medical Marketing Whiz. So far we are extremely happy. In one week we have added close to 50 followers on FB. Sherry, our account manager is extremely helpful, effective, very responsive, and most importantly very efficient and knowledgeable. I think with the way it's going we will achieve our goals in no time."
~ *Anteneh Roba*

Made in the USA
Monee, IL
02 March 2024